Jump In:
A Workbook for
Reluctant and Eager
Writers

Sharon Watson

Illustrations by Brett Sempsrott except where noted
Brett Sempsrott's illustrations digitized by Megan Whitaker
Illustrations on pp. 78,141 from www.clipart.com
Cover design by Kim Williams

Passages on pp. 164-165 from ANNE'S HOUSE OF DREAMS by L.M. Montgomery. New York: Bantam Books, 1998.

Passages on pp. 190, 193 from THE PHANTOM TOLLBOOTH by Norton Juster illustrated by Jules Feiffer, copyright © 1961 and renewed 1989 by Norton Juster; Illustrations copyright © 1961 and renewed 1989 by Jules Feiffer. Used by permission of Random House Children's Books, a division of Random House, Inc.

All Bible quotations are from The New International Version.

ISBN 10: 1-932012-74-5
ISBN 13: 978-1-932012-74-3

Published by Apologia Educational Ministries, Inc.
1106 Meridian Plaza, Suite 220
Anderson, IN 46016
888-524-4724
www.apologia.com

To the mothers and students
who participated in my
Circuit-Riding Teacher Classes,
to Terry,
and to my three original students,
upon whom I experimented freely.

Table of Contents

11/30/09

Getting Your Feet Wet

Skill 1: Treading **Water**

Writing may send warm shivers of pleasure up your spine. Or it may make you feel as though you are drowning in an angry, choppy, icy sea with nothing in sight but hungry, toothy sharks and storm clouds spitting out stony hail as big as rotten eggs.

Either way, this workbook is going to make writing easier for you. Really.

Now it's your turn.   Answer the questions below and on the next page. No one will grade your answers, so be honest.

1. What types of writing assignments are difficult for you?

    All of them

2. What are the easiest writing assignments?

    Poems, and Childrens stories

3. If you could write anything, what would you write?

    A story about rabbits that talk

4. What is a hard thing about writing? What is an easy thing?

The hard thing is motivating

The easy thing is thinking of ideas

Turn to page 235 and look in **YOUR LOCKER.** There you will find *Writing from Beginning to End*, **Mistake Medic**, and other helpful tools. **Mistake Medic** is essential; you will need it for every assignment. Use this stuff—it's yours!

Now go to the next page and fill out the quick questionnaire you find there.

It's all about ME!

Writing is better…

(Check **all** the boxes below that finish the above sentence and are true for you. ⬇)

☐ in the morning.   ☐ at a desk.

☑ if I choose the topic.   ☑ near a window.

☑ on my bed.   ☑ when I write stories.

☐ with other people.   ☐ at the computer.

☐ when I have my cat or dog in the room.   ☐ outside.

☐ in a chair. ☑ when I have lots of time. ☑ late at night.

☐ at the kitchen table.   ☐ with a pencil.

☑ if I get to write my opinion about something.

☐ when I research for reports.   ☐ on the floor.

☑ when it's quiet. ☑ when I'm alone.   ☐ with music.

☑ with a pen.   ☐ in a beanbag chair.

☐ if someone tells me what to write.

☐ at the same time every day.   ☐ I don't know.

☑ when I know I will not be graded on it.

▶ Have you learned anything about yourself? Pay attention to when you like to write and where you like to write. It will make writing sooo much easier!

Skill 2: **Stop!** Don't write yet!

Suppose your teacher gives you an assignment to write a report on a recent natural disaster, and you get to choose which disaster. There are many from which to choose. Quickly list possible natural disasters you could write about. The first two are done for you.

1. flood
2. fire
3. earthquake
4. hurricane
5. tornado
6. apocalypse
7. El Niño
8. La Niña

What you just did is called **brainstorming**; you wrote down ideas as they came to you. You didn't write them in any particular order. You just wrote words as they popped into your head.

Brainstorm ideas before you write any assignment. You will not use all the ideas you list, but you will use many of them. Brainstorming is a good way to get you thinking about the subject (topic). It will make writing your assignment so much easier.

Think about this: Suppose you decide to write your report on an earthquake. What are some of the things you will include in your report? What are some of the things you are going to have to find out about before you write? Where do you begin? You brainstorm.

There are lots of ways to brainstorm. You've already used the **number method** (above). Another way is to write your ideas anywhere on a piece of paper. Or you can make a list with **dashes** or **bullets**, like this:

-- In what country was the earthquake?
-- Where was the epicenter?
-- What was its number on the Richter scale?
-- What happened to the people (how were they affected)?
-- (You will keep writing ideas.)

OR

- In what country was the earthquake?
- Where was the epicenter?

- What was its number on the Richter scale?
- What happened to the people (how were they affected)?
- (You will keep writing ideas.)

Another interesting method you can use for brainstorming is called the **cluster method**. Your drawing will look much like a solar system; the topic goes in the middle (like the sun), and your ideas revolve around your topic (like the planets). Other smaller ideas may be attached to larger ideas (like satellites or moons around the planets). Below is one example of the *cluster method* of brainstorming. Read it and then turn the page.

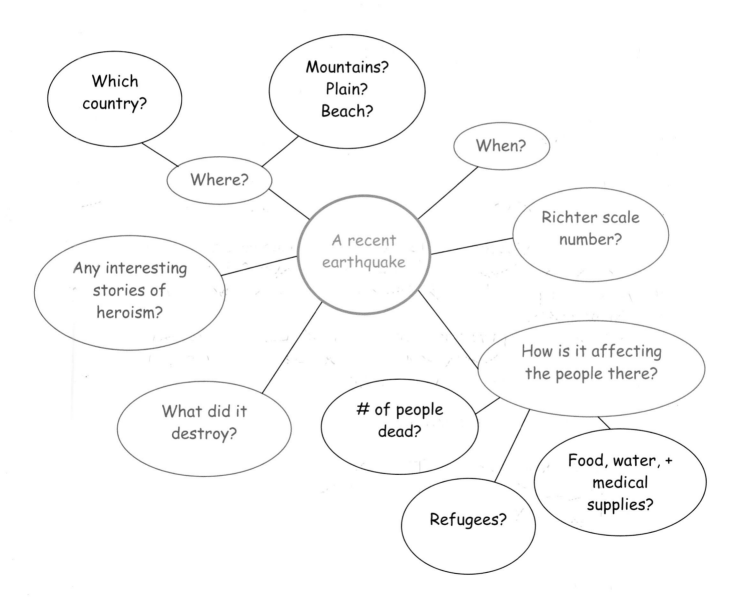

Now it's your turn. Which method of brainstorming did you like the best? Check the box next to your favorite method for organizing your thoughts.

☑ Making a list anywhere on the paper   ☐ Using bullets
☐ Using numbers   ☑ Using the cluster method
☐ Using dashes

Now it's your turn again. Decide which natural disaster you are going to brainstorm for a report (you won't really be writing the report—just writing down ideas for one). Choose a disaster other than an earthquake.

The natural disaster: _Hurricane_

Now brainstorm ideas for what you might include in your report. Remember, they're just ideas; write lots of them now, even if they seem silly. Use your favorite method and the space below.

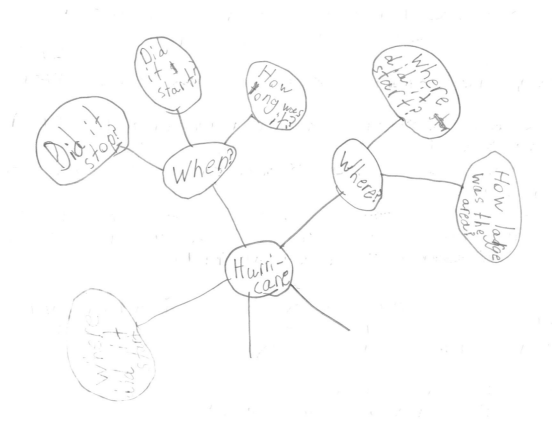

Skill 3: Make it **Easy** on yourself

Writing uses two distinct and separate skills:

- Putting the words down on paper (creating)

- Fixing the words, grammar, punctuation, paragraphs, spelling, sentence structure and lengths, etc. (proofreading)

It is too hard to do both at once—they happen in two different parts of your brain. Even seasoned professional writers don't do both skills at the same time. They know that once they get their words down on paper, they can go back and fix them later. If they agonized over everything they wrote, wondering if they were doing it right, they would never get anything written.

And neither will you.

Here is good advice: Just write! Keep the pencil moving. Keep the thoughts flowing from your brain to the keyboard or pen. If you think that what you are writing is stupid or isn't making any sense or isn't grammatically correct, don't sweat it. Just write! You can go back later and fix it.

Don't agonize over a bad first sentence. Keep writing. You can fix it later.

Use one skill at a time. First write; then fix.

Don't stop and look up a word you think you misspelled. Circle it and fix it later.

Don't reread your first sentences and weep and wail because they are horrible. Keep writing; you can fix them later. When you are creating your writing assignment, turn off your internal editor who tells you that your writing is awful.

When do you turn the editor back on? When you proofread, proofread, proofread (that means "proofread three times!") **after** you have written your assignment. Each paper needs three separate proofreading sessions.

Now it's your turn. Turn off your internal editor. **Choose** one of the topics below and **write** on the next page for ten minutes. No one will grade it. Start the timer when you begin to write—and keep writing!

1. Write about the best day you've ever had. OR
2. Write about a pet peeve or a character trait you can't stand.

TEN MINUTES: Yesterday was the best day ever. First I did most of my school in the morning. Then, at 12:30, we went ice skating. After that I finished school and played computer. Around 4:00 I went to my friends house and played over there for a bit. Finnaly, I went to swim practice with my other friends. Lastly, I went home and went to bed.

THE END time: 1 and a left: half minute

Opinions—You've Got Them!

Skill 1: What do you **Think?**

Writing your opinion is only slightly different than *saying* your opinion. And you say your opinions all the time! An opinion can come from something you can't stand or something you love. In other words, you feel strongly about it, one way or another.

You probably have an opinion on what kind of student you are, what book or movie your best friend would love, which Bible story or verse is your favorite, or what you want to eat for your next snack. All of those are opinions—and you have them!

Now it's your turn. Brainstorm by filling in the blanks that interest you. There are more on the next page.

My Favorite	The Worst (least favorite)
Color _green_	_red_
Ice cream flavor _gumball_	_pistachio_
Sports team _giants_	

Song ___Its the end of the world as we know it___ _____

Book ___The tale of Despereaux___ ___Pony Pals___

Car _____ _____

Activity ___ice skating___ ___school___

School subject ___reading___ ___writing___

Animal ___Cavy___ ___all birds___

Outfit ___T-shirt and shorts___ ___long sleeved shirt and Jeans___

Store ___target ◎___ ___Costco___

Meal ___mac and cheese___ ___beans___

Vacation _____ _____

Game ___Super monkeyball___ ___Lego Indiana Jones___

Complete these sentences:

My favorite song is ___its the end of the world as we know it.___

The worst sports team in the world is _____.

Congratulations! You have just written your opinion.

Skill 2: What about the **Why?**

Any opinion, no matter how well it is written, must have **reasons**. You have to say why you believe in your opinion so people can agree with you and care about it.

Read the two conversations below. In them, Luke and Jessica are giving their reasons for their opinions. See if you can catch the reasons:

Juan: What about that game last night?

Luke: It stank! They kept missing the rebounds, they couldn't keep a decent zone defense, and Jones was benched in the first quarter with an injury. What a mess!

Kristen: So, how is it? How do I look in it?

Jessica: That is *so you!* You look great in that color, and it's the perfect size. Now hurry up! I want to try it on too.

Now it's your turn. Think about a time when you told someone your opinion. Try to remember what your reasons were. Write your opinion and your reasons in the space below. Then turn the page.

OPINION:

Cavies are good pets.

REASONS:

1. cavies seldom bite.

2. cavies love to snuggle with their human owners

3. they are fuzzy and small.

Notice that in the examples on the previous page, each person gave three reasons for the opinion. Luke mentioned the bad rebounding, the lousy zone defense, and an injured player. Jessica said it was a good color, the right size, and desirable as a fashion. Find the reasons given in the next conversation (in the box below):

CARL: I'm going to play baseball with one of the teams in town this summer. What about you?

JON: Not me. I'm going to concentrate on soccer. In fact, I want to play on a professional team someday.

CARL: Professional? Oh, right—you broke the league record for goals in a season, didn't you?

JON: Yeah. You know, when I'm running down the field, it's almost like I'm flying. When I wake up in the morning, I can't wait to put on my cleats and hit the field. I practice at home at least four hours a day. It's like I was born to play soccer.

CARL: So, what do your parents think about all of this?

JON: Oh, they're for it. Coach Hamm came to our house last week and talked to them. We figured out a practice schedule. They're all pulling for me.

Now it's your turn again. Jon clearly believes he will make a professional soccer team someday. That is his opinion of his abilities. What are the three reasons that came up in this conversation?

1. His parents and coach are supporting him

2. he likes to play the sport

3. he broke a league record

Skill 3: A good **Order**

In any well-written opinion, you should have at least three good reasons to support your opinion. But wait—there's more! You should also *arrange your reasons in an interesting order.* There are many ways to do this that will hold the reader's interest. You will learn two in this skill. Read the examples below:

Jon thinks he can get on a professional team. Why?

Jon thinks he can get on a professional team. Why?

1. **Most important:** He proved his talent by breaking a league record.
2. **Next important:** His coach and parents see his talent and are supporting him.
3. **Least important:** He loves to play the sport.

1. **Next important:** His coach and parents see his talent and are supporting him.
2. **Least important:** He loves to play the sport.
3. **But most important:** He proved his talent by breaking a league record.

Do you agree that the most important reason is that he broke the league record? Do you agree that the least important reason is that he loves to play soccer? Or is the fact that he loves to play the biggest reason? If you think one reason is more important than another, it is your job to make it more important by what you say about it!

Whatever you do, don't begin with your least important reason. You will lose your reader right away!

Now it's your turn. You listed many opinions in Skill 1, pages 13 and 14. Choose one of those now or choose a new one and write it on the next page. Then brainstorm five reasons why you like or don't like that particular thing. Don't pay attention to the most important or least important right now. Just write down your reasons as they come to you. Remember: write now, fix later.

Opinion: Lego Indiana Jones is the worst game ever

Reasons:

___ 1. The game is boring.

___ 2. ~~can~~ the game can be beaten ~~in~~ in a day.

___ 3. ~~Its not theirs no four~~ not ment for lots of people. be played over again.

___ 4. not ment to

___ 5. ~~no fun~~

Look back over your list and cross off the two weakest reasons or the reasons you think you might not be able to write much about.

In the blanks next to the remaining three reasons, write MI for your most important reason, NI for your next important reason, and LI for your least important reason.

Select the order in which you want to use your reasons by underlining one of these sets:

most important, next important, least important order

OR

next important, least important, most important order

In the blanks below, rearrange your three reasons from above in the new order you just selected.

1. not ment for lots of people

2. it can be beaten in a day

3. boring if you play it twice.

Now you have a good skeleton to use for the body of your opinion paper. In Skill 4, you will put some flesh on those bones.

Skill 4: The **Body**

Each reason lives in its own paragraph. Because you're using three reasons, the middle part (the body) of your opinion paper will have three paragraphs. Each reason also has to have a few supporting statements to make it strong, like pilings under a bridge. The supporting statements are usually facts or examples. Read the following paper, "My New Pet," to see how this works. Note the order the reasons are in.

Introduction ▶
(see Skill 5, p. 21,22)

Reason # one ▶
(most important)

Reason # two ▶
(next important)

Reason # three ▶
(least important)

Conclusion ▶
(see Skill 6, p. 23-25)

My New Pet

When my mom said I could have a pet, I went to the pet store to look at all the animals. Which one did I choose? I saw the cute gerbils and hamsters scurrying in their cages. I listened to the canaries, parakeets, and finches singing. I watched the three fuzzy puppies playing with a ball. But when I came to the kitten cage, I knew what I wanted.

Cats are clean. They are constantly licking themselves to remove burrs, dirt, and unpleasant smells. Cats can be trained to use a kitty litter box, making it easy to clean up after them.

Cats are smart. They cover up their messes. And if you happen to miss a day feeding your cats, it is only a small problem to them. They know how to find mice, moles, small rabbits, and even moths for their meals.

Cats are polite. They quietly walk through the house, minding their own business. They are not fussy, and they have manners.

I chose a white and butterscotch kitten, and I named her Sundae. Mom bought a scratching post so Sundae would have a safe place to sharpen her claws. I bought a little ball with a bell inside it so Sundae could have something to play with. She's the cutest thing! She's a fluffy ball of fur. I loved having a kitten so much that I went back the next day and bought Chocolate, her sister. Now I have two pets, and I love them both!

Notice that all the reasons turned into **topic sentences** (what the rest of the paragraph is about).

Now it's your turn.   All of the reasons for buying a cat have at least two supporting statements. List the two things the writer used to prove that cats are clean.

1. They are constahtly licking themselves to remove burrs, dirt, and odors.

2. They can be trained to use a kitty litter box.

On page 18 (Skill 3), you chose three reasons for your own opinion. CHOOSE **ONE** of those reasons now and fill out a paragraph with supporting statements.

Reason (which becomes your topic sentence):

Lego Indiana Jones is not for lots of people.

Supporting statements for reason (the rest of the paragraph):

It can only have two people play at the same time, which doesn't make a good game for big families. Its not focused toward older children, so its not as fun as it could be.

Skill 5: **Hello!**

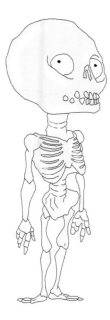

Even a skeleton needs a head. The **introductory paragraph** will become your skeleton's head.

The first sentence in your *introductory paragraph* (or introduction) should grab the reader's attention. If soccer-playing Jon wrote a report on why he thought he could get on a professional team, he wouldn't begin it like this: "This is a report on why I will someday play soccer on a professional team." If he did, you would start snoozing.

Your job is to grab the reader's interest by beginning with a bang. You do this by using an interesting statement, fact, quotation, question, or story.

- **An interesting statement:** All my life I've only had one goal—to play soccer on a professional team.

- **An interesting fact:** A professional soccer team has only eleven players on the field. Someday, I'm going to be one of them.

- **A quotation:** "Feet, knees, chest, head—no matter how Jon handles the ball, he does it right," Coach Hamm told my parents last night.

- **A question:** What does it take to earn a spot on a professional soccer team?

- **A story:** When I was five years old, my dad took me to a sporting-goods store. As we walked up and down the aisles, I saw baseballs, basketballs, and footballs in their fancy boxes. I noticed yellow tennis balls in their tubes. Then I saw a round ball with interesting black and white geometric shapes all over it. When I asked my dad what it was, he took it out of the box and handed it to me. From the moment the leather hit my skin, I was hooked.

Remember to include your **opinion** in your introduction. Don't keep it a surprise.

Here's an example of an opinion in an introductory paragraph, which uses an interesting quotation:

> According to an ad by the oil company Chevron, "It took us 125 years to use the first trillion barrels of oil. We'll use the next trillion in 30." Clearly, it's time to conserve some natural resources.

The writer's opinion is the last sentence: "Clearly, it's time to conserve some natural resources." The student will most likely continue on with different natural resources and how to conserve them, finishing with how the reader can conserve too.

Here's another example of an introductory paragraph. It is from an opinion paper written by a boy in the eighth grade:

> Wind blowing through your hair at 231 mph is an everyday experience for some people. No, I'm not talking about the latest hairdryer or the world's fastest roller-coaster ride or even a Ferrari. I'm talking about the world's fastest production car, the McLaren F1.

Notice that he began with an interesting statement. Also notice that he did not write, "I like the McLaren F1." He didn't have to. You know his opinion of the car by how exciting he made it sound in his *interesting statement*.

Make sure these three ingredients are swimming around in your introduction: an interesting beginning, the topic, and your opinion of the topic. If the reader doesn't know the topic and your opinion of it by the end of the first paragraph, check your "recipe" to see what you left out.

Now it's your turn. Write an introduction for your opinion in the space below. Begin it by using any of the five tools listed on page 21. Make sure the reader knows whether you are for or against the topic.

Some games are bad, like Eragon and Simcity Creator, but I think one of the worst is Lego Indiana Jones.

Skill 6: **Goodbye!**

If the skeleton's head is your introduction, then the skeleton's feet are the **conclusion**.

Avoid just restating all your reasons for your opinion in your *concluding paragraph* (conclusion).   That's a snoozer too.   Tell the reader something of interest about the subject without introducing another point.   Again, use an interesting statement, fact, quotation, question, or story you've saved for the end.   Here are some examples Jon could use for his conclusion:

- **An interesting statement:** It takes a lot of hard work to get on a professional team. It takes a powerful dream too. And it takes an encouraging support team. I know I'll make it because I've got all three.

- **An interesting fact:** Before you tell me that my professional dreams are ridiculous, remember the famous skier that put our town on the map in the last Olympics. If she can make it from this small town, so can I. And I intend to!

- **A quotation:** At our annual awards dinner, the president of the Mountain City Soccer League said, "I think we have another Pelé on our hands." He was referring to me. I'm not there yet, but I intend to be.

- **A question:** Our town's famous skier received the key to the city at the end of her homecoming parade. When I turn professional and help win the World Cup for the U.S. soccer team, will Mountain City do the same for me?

- **A story:** I dream about the team, the practices, and the hard work it will take to get on a professional team. As a five-year-old boy, I had no idea that my first soccer ball would take me so far. But that little kid dreamed big. And I still do.

Get the picture? Below, read how the eighth-grade boy concluded his opinion paper on the McLaren F1. He used interesting statements:

> Obviously the McLaren F1 wins the race against the Ferrari 550 Maranello because of its size, weight, and performance. No wonder the McLaren F1 is the world's fastest production car! Next time you want to take a joy ride, choose a McLaren F1—and skip the roller coaster!

Any time you can tie your conclusion to your introduction, you give your reader a satisfying experience. Notice that when the writer mentioned the roller coaster in his conclusion, he was tying that paragraph to his introduction.

> Tying your conclusion to your introduction is called the full-circle technique.

Now it's your turn. Write a satisfying conclusion to your opinion in the space below. Use any of the five tools listed on page 23. When you finish, read the next page.

~~Like~~ My brother be~~lives~~

~~"This~~ game ~~really stinks" and so do~~

~~I.~~ ~~X~~ My brother quotes,

"This game is awful, I ~~wound~~

would'nt play it in a million

years," and I for one, agree

with him.

⇨   Here's something interesting: You didn't begin at the top of a blank piece of paper and write to the bottom of it. Look at the process you've already gone through:

- **Brainstorm**. You listed some of your opinions and chose one to work with.

- **Prewrite.** You listed five reasons for the opinion you chose. Then you crossed off two that were weak or that wouldn't work.

- **Order.** You chose a logical order in which to present your reasons.

- **Write the body.** You wrote supporting statements for one of your three reasons. If you were writing this opinion, you would finish the other two paragraphs.

- **Write the introduction.** You thought of an interesting statement, fact, quotation, question, or story with which to begin your introduction. You made sure the reader knew your topic, and you included your opinion.

- **Write the conclusion.** You thought of an interesting statement, fact, quotation, question, or story to include in your conclusion. You filled in more to finish out the paragraph if you needed to. You tried to tie your conclusion to your introduction in some way.

Although you began your writing with the body, you may begin at the introduction or even the conclusion if you wish. Some professional writers begin with the conclusion because they know how they want their report to end. For most writers of your age, however, it is best to begin with the body or the introduction.

What's left? If you were going to finish this opinion, you would put the introduction, body, and conclusion in the right order. Then you would proofread, proofread, proofread (that means "Proofread Three Times!") using the **Mistake Medic** on page 238. And last, you would hand a polished paper to your teacher and relax.

Skill 7 has a copy of a real opinion paper on it. It's about...well, you can read it and find out.

Skill 7: An interesting **Friend**

A girl in the fifth grade wrote this opinion. It contains 243 words and a very interesting friend. Read it and answer the questions at the end.

My Friend

Every Friday, I carry my peg-legged friend up the stairs to the door of Mrs. Westfield's small home covered in vines. Don't worry. My friend isn't a pirate. She's a cello.

I found my beloved friend four years ago on an old, white shelf at Mrs. Westfield's home. She dusted her off and told me to take good care of her, for she would be my friend for the rest of my life. I have loved playing the cello from the very beginning.

The cello is known for its deep, rich sound. It is fun to shift up and down the fingerboard. In orchestra, the cello often plays the harmony part. I also like learning about different composers such as Bach and Mozart and reading about famous musicians such as Yo-Yo Ma and Pablo Casals.

Mrs. Westfield makes it so enjoyable; without her I think I would have lost hope by now. She makes learning so much fun by using different, easy techniques. Mrs. Westfield has always been understanding. She doesn't get angry if I make a mistake but encourages me to try again.

The most exciting part of playing the cello is performing. I have enjoyed playing in duets, trios, quartets, music camps, nursing homes, church, and recitals.

I encourage you to play the cello, too, or at least try. Who knows? You may make a life-long friend. I know I'll never part with my peg-legged friend.

Now it's your turn. Answer the following questions:

1. Does she have an interesting first sentence?

Yes

2. How does she tie her conclusion to her introduction?

She refers to the cello as her peg-legged friend

3. In paragraphs four and five, what are her reasons for liking the cello?

Paragraph 4: *her teacher makes it enjoyable*

Paragraph 5: *She likes performing*

4. After reading this, do you think you would like to play the cello?

Yes

Skill 8: The **Assignment**

CHOOSE **ONE**:

☐ Complete and polish the opinion you have been working on. Word count: at least 150 words.

☑ Do you love to write? Don't like to write? Couldn't care one way or the other about writing? Write your opinion of writing. Use at least 150 words.

☐ The writer of "My New Pet" really likes cats. Do you disagree with the writer? Is there another animal you like better? Write your opinion of that animal. Or write why you detest cats! Use at least 150 words.

☐ Look at the favorite/worst lists you filled out on pages 13 and 14 (in Skill 1). Choose one of those topics and write your opinion about it in at least 150 words.

☐ Your choice. Choose something that you love or can't stand (something you feel strongly about) and write your opinion of it. Use at least 150 words.

A suggested writing schedule:

Day 1 ► Brainstorm. Decide on your opinion, your three reasons, and an order in which to put them.

Days 2-3 ► Write the body (the three paragraphs that include your three reasons).

Day 4 ► Write the introduction and conclusion.

Day 5 ► Put the paragraphs in the right order. Proofread three separate times for mistakes. Make a neat copy.

Persuasion: The Basics

Skill 1: Words can be **Powerful**

In 1830, a young man learned that a famous ship was scheduled to be dismantled. The warship *Constitution* had won some important battles in the War of 1812, and it seemed a shame to this young man to destroy such history. What did he do? Did he stand on the street corners and shout his opinion? Did he write fiery letters to Congress? Did he begin a campaign to collect enough money to save her?

A poem saved a ship from destruction!

No, he did none of those things. Instead, he used his frustration to write a poem of three stanzas (verses), and he sent it to his local newspaper. They printed it. The poem became so popular that it was reprinted in newspapers all across the nation. Did it work? Did he save the ship?

Yes, he did. You may see the *Constitution* in Boston today, sitting in the Charleston Navy Yard. She is a floating museum. What was the little poem that saved a piece of United States history? "Old Ironsides" by Oliver Wendell Holmes. He was twenty-one when he wrote that poem.

Writing a persuasive paper is a step beyond writing your opinion. When you wrote your **opinion**, you stated what you were for or against, and you explained why. The following sentences are examples of opinions:

- I can't stand the Chicago Bears.
- My best friend is Rosa.

Those are simply opinions. If you were writing a paper on either one of those opinions, you would give good reasons why you don't like the Bears or why you like Rosa.

When you write a **persuasive** paper, however, you are trying to persuade the reader to do these two things:

- **Believe** a certain way
- **Behave** a certain way

By the end of your paper, you want your reader to think a certain way about your topic. You want to change your reader's mind! And you want your reader to behave in a certain way by acting differently or by doing something.

Now it's your turn. Believe it or not, you try to persuade people all the time. Think of the last time you tried to talk a parent, a friend, or a brother or sister into thinking or acting a certain way. Was it about permission to go to that concert? Was it to get someone to share something with you? What was it? Answer the following questions.

What did you want that person to think or do (believe or behave)?

What were your reasons?

1.

2.

3.

Oliver Wendell Holmes tried to get people to believe that the ship was worth saving and behave (act) in a way that would save the ship.

Skill 2: What's it all **About?**

Your mission is to convince your reader to believe and behave a certain way. So, what's the **topic**? What's the subject of your paper? If it is up to you, choose something that you **feel strongly about**. There's no sense wasting your time writing about why all girls should dress in pink all the time if you don't care about perpetually pink-clothed girls. Here are some things you may feel strongly about:

- Recycling
- Abortion
- The humane treatment of animals
- Why you are the best person to play a certain position on your team
- War
- The minimum driving age of teens
- Why your friend should listen to you about Jesus
- Pirating songs off the Internet
- Why your friend should see or not see a particular movie

Now it's your turn. Make a list below of things that you feel strongly about, things that you want people to **think** a certain way about or **do** something about.

1.

2.

3.

4.

Choose one of those topics and circle it. Then turn the page.

Now decide what you want the reader to think and do about it.

For instance, if your topic is recycling, how do you want your reader to respond to your paper? Do you want him to...

- sort plastic and glass from his own garbage and take it to the curb or to the special recycling bins around town?
- be convinced that your town needs to put recycling bins in the parking lots of popular stores?
- write letters to the mayor about getting public recycling bins?

It's up to you. You have to decide what your goal is. You have to decide what you want the reader to think or do.

Remember, you will want to change your reader's beliefs **and** behaviors. For instance, the mayor will not change his behavior (putting up recycling bins around town) until he has also changed his beliefs about recycling.

Now it's your turn again. In the space below, write what you want your reader to think and do about the topic you chose (what beliefs and behaviors you want to change). This becomes your **purpose statement**. It will not appear in your paper, but it will guide all that you decide to write. Remember not only to try to change his mind but also give him something to do.

Example: By the end of my paper, I want to convince the readers that recycling is the right thing to do and that they should sort their own recyclables and put them in the special bins around town.

By the end of my paper, I want to convince my reader _____

_____

_____

_____

Skill 3: Gimme a good **Reason**

Pretend that you have just watched a great video or read a great book. You want your library to have a copy of it so other students can enjoy it. Or pretend you have just watched a horrible video or read a horrible book. In that case, you want your library *never* to buy it.

(By the way, *video* here means a movie, a short video like one of a VeggieTales or Odyssey series, or an educational video. You have a lot of options.)

Choose the video or book and write the title and author in the blanks below.

Title: _____

Author, if necessary: _____

Your *purpose statement* for writing this letter is this: By the end of my letter, I want to convince the librarian to buy this video or book (or never buy it).

When the librarian gets your letter, she doesn't just want to know how much you liked the video or book (or didn't like it). She wants to know all your **reasons** why you thought it was good (or bad) and why other students will want to check it out (or not).

Now it's your turn. List five reasons why you thought it was a great/horrible video or book and why other kids will want (or not want) to check it out too. In other words, list five reasons why the library should buy (or not buy) this video or book.

1.

2.

3.

4.

5.

Skill 4: **Order** up!

You now have five reasons why the library should buy (or not buy) the video or book. Go back to page 33 and cross off two weak ones. The next thing to do is to arrange the three remaining reasons in a usable order. Below is an example of a book, a purpose statement, and three reasons why the library should buy this book:

Book: *Out of the Dust* by Karen Hesse

Purpose statement: By the end of this letter, I want the librarian to be convinced to buy this book for the library.

Reasons: 1. Even though it is in non-rhyming poetry, it is easy to understand.
2. I learned a lot about the Dust Bowl in Oklahoma in the 1930s.
3. I learned how important it is to forgive.

In order to write to this librarian, you will put your reasons in a logical order. The reasons to buy the book *Out of the Dust* are currently in this order: least important, next important, most important. But you don't want to write about them in that order. Who would keep reading if you put your least important reason first?

There are many correct ways to put your reasons in a good order. Below are two good ways to arrange them. You may remember them from page 17 ("Opinions—You've Got Them!") The order you choose should make your reasons look the best they can.

1. **Most** important: I learned how important it is to forgive.
2. **Next** important: I learned a lot about the Dust Bowl in Oklahoma in the 1930s.
3. **Least** important: Even though it is written in non-rhyming poetry, it is easy to understand.

1. **Next** important: I learned a lot about the Dust Bowl in Oklahoma in the 1930s.
2. **Least** important: Even though it is written in non-rhyming poetry, it is easy to understand.
3. But **Most** important: I learned how important it is to forgive.

Now it's your turn. Determine the importance of your three remaining reasons from page 33 (Skill 3) and put them in the order of most important, next important, and least important.

1. Most important:

2. Next important:

3. Least important:

Now that you have determined which reasons are most, next, and least important, put them in the following order:

1. Next important:

2. Least important:

3. Most important:

Compare your two lists. Which seems the best order for your points? You, the writer, will determine this for each persuasive paper you write. You will usually choose the order that best helps your purpose statement. The order may be different in different papers or you may grow to like one order over another. Use your instincts—your gut feeling. Remember your audience; they are the people whose minds you are trying to change. Which way, with your particular set of reasons, packs a bigger punch? It's up to you to decide.

Skill 5: Oh, **Yeah?**

As you could have guessed, each reason gets its own paragraph. What do you put in the rest of the paragraph? You fill it with items that support your reason, like legs on a dog.

To support your reasons, you can choose from a variety of tools. Here are some ideas:

- **Facts** that prove your point
- A **story** that relates to your point
- Logical **statements** that show the rightness of your point
- A small **quotation** to show that an expert agrees with you
- **Examples** that prove your point

Imagine that you feel strongly that your town should have a skate park. One of your reasons could be that skating is healthful. But now you need to prove it. You need to support it. Choose some tools to fill in the paragraph and persuade your reader. Here are some examples of ways to use your tools:

- ◆ **Facts:** Skating is healthful. Jimmy, who was twenty pounds overweight, lost all his extra pounds and got into good shape by skating. And since Vanetta's been skating, she has enough stamina to run on her cross-country team.

- ◆ A **story:** Skating is healthful. Nicole hated any physical exercise and was always tired. When she went to her doctor, she learned that she could cure her fatigue herself. All she needed to do was to find an activity that she liked (running, walking, horseback riding, volleyball, skating, etc.) and do it for twenty minutes a day. She chose skating. Now she feels good and isn't tired any more.

- ◆ Logical **statements:** Skating is healthful. It can increase your metabolism, get your heart pumping, and build your muscles. Kids who have skated for a while can tell you that they are stronger today than they were a year ago. Sitting at home with a video game won't do that for you unless you just want strong thumbs.

- ◆ A **quotation:** Skating is healthful. Dr. Cynthia Grey, a local pediatrician, says, "Skateboarding gets kids outdoors in the fresh air and provides hours of great exercise. In an age of overweight children, skating makes a fun way for them to improve their heart health and get into shape."

♦ **Examples:** Skating is healthful.   The skater is in constant motion.   That increases stamina.   It takes a lot of strength to perform a Caballerial or a McTwist.   It takes a lot of coordination, too.   Skating gets teens outdoors and away from the television, video games, and junk food.   It's a physical activity that will help them become healthier adults.

Notice that the point or topic sentence is the same in each of these tools: "Skating is healthful." Each tool, however, gave the point a different meaning or a different slant. Some tools are very similar to each other.   Don't sweat the differences—just keep writing and proving your point!

Which one would you choose for the "Skating is healthful" point?

Now it's your turn. Choose **one** of the following:

❑ On page 31 (Skill 2), you circled a topic.   On page 32, you wrote a purpose statement for it.   Think of one reason you could use to persuade your reader.   Then write the reason and supporting statements below.   Use one or more of the above tools in your paragraph.

❑ On page 33 (Skill 3), you chose a great/horrible video or book.   You also selected three reasons to include in your letter.   Choose one reason now and write it below. Then fill in the supporting statements. Use one or more of the above tools in your paragraph.

Reason (which becomes the topic sentence):

Supporting statements (the rest of the paragraph):

Skill 6: The bread for the Sandwich

If the three reasons (or points) are the filling to the sandwich you are building, then the introduction and the conclusion are the top and bottom pieces of bread that hold the sandwich together.

Your **introduction** is one paragraph long and must introduce your reader to the topic.

Make sure that your first sentence is interesting enough to keep the reader reading. It is your job to hook the reader's attention by using a **statement**, **fact**, **quotation**, **question**, or **story**. Turn to pages 21 and 22 (Opinions, Skill 5) to review any of these.

In your first paragraph, also include which side of the topic you are on—whether you are for it or against it. For example:

- You don't have to write, "I support a skate park," or "I am against a skate park." You can use a statement like this: "I hope our town will give us teens permission to build a skate park on the site of the old Peterson warehouse." That way everyone will know which side of the issue you are on, and it shows you have been thinking about it in a helpful way.

- In the letter to the librarian about the great/horrible video or book, you don't have to write, "I liked the book." If you write that you hope the library will buy the book so other readers can enjoy this wonderful story, the words *enjoy* and *wonderful* will tell the librarian very clearly that you liked the book.

Now it's your turn. In the space below, write a short introductory paragraph for the topic you wrote the supporting statements for on page 37 (in Skill 5).

The **conclusion** (the last paragraph) is your last chance to change the reader's mind and behavior.

This is it! You won't get another chance. So don't blow it by restating everything you already said elsewhere. Come up with an interesting way to sway your reader. This is not the place to introduce a new point.

In addition to an interesting **statement, fact, quotation, question,** or **story,** use a **call to action** in your conclusion. This is your chance to challenge your reader to *do something* (change his behavior). That's what a *call to action* means. Give the reader something positive and specific to do.

This is the **wrong** way to finish your persuasive paper:

> So, I think a skate park will help teens be healthier, it will give us a nice place to go, and it will teach us to be more responsible because we will be running it. That's why we need a new skate park.

Ouch! That was awful! Why? It lists all the points in your report, and it misses the chance to challenge your readers and give them something practical to do.

Here's a better way to finish your persuasive paper because it gives the reader something to **think about** and something constructive **to do:**

> The next time you see an overweight, out-of-shape teen, remember how a new skate park built on the site of the old Peterson warehouse could help him. Please attend the meeting in the mayor's office next Tuesday night at 7 p.m. to discuss this exciting possibility.

Whew! That was a lot better.

Now it's your turn again. In the space below, write an interesting but short concluding paragraph for the topic you wrote the introduction for. Remember to tie the conclusion to the introduction and give a call to action.

Skill 7: Does he Make the Grade?

A boy in the seventh grade wrote this persuasive paper. It contains 354 words. Read it and answer the questions on the next page.

Spider-Man Rocks

Action, excitement, suspense, a good story, and a nasty villain—these are the qualities of a good movie. Today there are too many movies with too much love, romance, bad language, and not enough action. If you want a good movie to watch, I urge you to watch *Spider-Man*.

Spider-Man has lots of action. It is always going from one action scene to another. It is never at a standstill; it just keeps moving. The scenes are clean too. They have almost no blood, and there are only a few bad words.

Spider-Man is the most exciting movie that I have seen. At the bridge scene, you can feel the terror of the kids, the decision of Spider-Man, and the triumph of the Green Goblin! It is an amazing scene. It makes you feel like you were there on the bridge. Some people say *Daredevil* had excitement. But whatever *Daredevil* had, *Spider-Man* has double.

They say suspense is something a movie must have to be a good movie. Well, if that's true, then *Spider-Man* is great. When I watch a movie, I don't like the beginning to give away the ending. *Spider-Man* keeps you on the edge of your seat through the whole movie.

In movies about superheroes, you want to know where they got their powers. In *Spider-Man*, you see him before he got his powers, and you see how he got his powers. If you want a good story and good action at the same time, *Spider-Man* is the movie for you.

One of the greatest keys to a good movie is having a strong villain. In *Spider-Man*, the villain is called the Green Goblin. If you ever have an audition for a nasty villain, this guy is your man. He means business. He wants Spider-Man dead, and he will stop at nothing to destroy him.

If you have seen *Spider-Man* and didn't like it, I strongly suggest that you watch it again with an open mind. If you have not seen *Spider-Man* and think it looks like a bad movie, I request that you watch it before you make any judgments.

Now it's your turn. Answer the questions on the next page.

1. Did his first sentence make you want to read more?

2. List the five reasons why he liked *Spider-Man*.

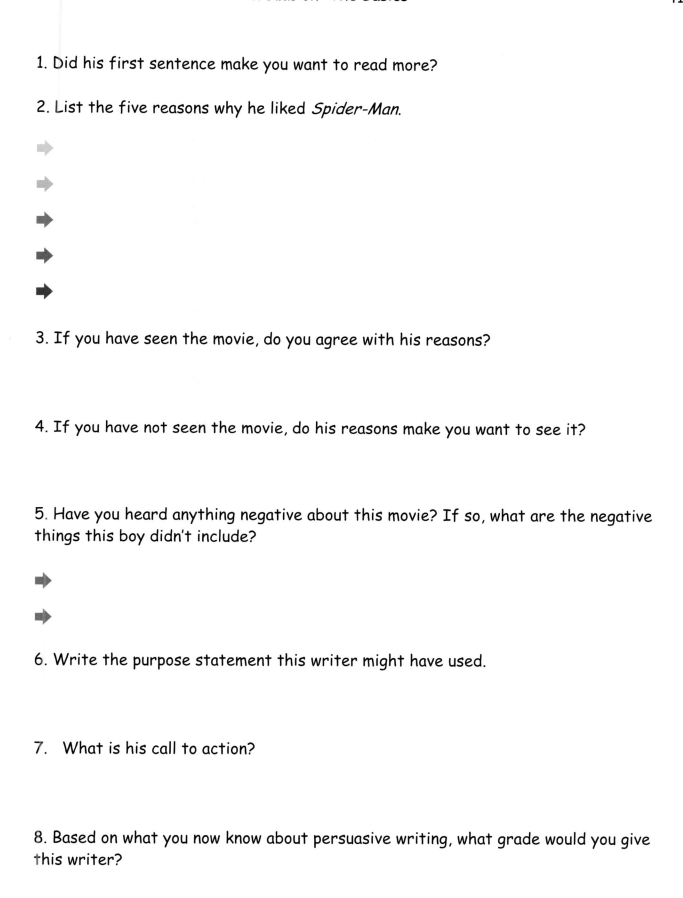

3. If you have seen the movie, do you agree with his reasons?

4. If you have not seen the movie, do his reasons make you want to see it?

5. Have you heard anything negative about this movie? If so, what are the negative things this boy didn't include?

6. Write the purpose statement this writer might have used.

7.   What is his call to action?

8. Based on what you now know about persuasive writing, what grade would you give this writer?

Skill 8: Get out the **Hammer!**

It is amazing but true that if you mention an **opposing view** in your paper, you will make your opinion even stronger. You do this by writing the opposite view fairly and then writing why it isn't right. Watch how this works in the examples below. This one is about abortion:

> Abortion counselors say that abortion is harmless to the woman. However, we now know that abortions are linked to depression, miscarriages in later pregnancies, and premature births in otherwise normal pregnancies.

This one is about a skate park:

> Some parents are afraid that their children will get hurt in a skate park. They say a skate park could be a dangerous place. But listen to what Dr. Cynthia Grey, a local pediatrician, has to say about it: "When a teen uses the proper protective gear, he or she is safer at a skate park than in the car with an older brother driving. I've seen skating accidents, and I've seen car accidents. Trust me. There is no comparison." Protective gear is the key to making the skate park safe.

This particular tool is so powerful, it is like a hammer. It tells the reader that you understand the arguments for and against the issue. It also tells the reader that you have done your research homework. And, most important, you get to mention the argument so you can refute it (prove it wrong).

You won't need it in every persuasive paper you write. Most often you will use it for a controversial issue (something people don't always agree on) like abortion, a skate park, homosexual marriages, etc. You won't need the hammer when you write your letter to the librarian unless the video or book is controversial. No one uses a hammer to fix a delicate watch!

Now it's your turn. Pretend you strongly believe that all students should eat a chocolate bar every day. Now pretend you have a friend who believes they shouldn't. What reason could your friend give to support this opposite belief? Write that reason on the next page.

Because you strongly believe that all students should eat a chocolate bar a day, your job is to prove your friend's reason wrong by using logic, a quotation, a fact, examples, or a story. Use the space below.

Skill 9: Persuasion **Wrongs** and **Rights**

Every game you play has its own set of rules. Persuasive writing does too. Read the **DON'T LIST** and the **DO LIST** below and on the next pages. If ya wanna win the game, ya gotta play by the rules.

DON'T LIST

1. **Don't insult** or single out a person or an entire group.
Wrong: Did you kids even look at yourselves in the mirror before you left the house? You're a mess!

2. **Don't wander** off your subject.
Wrong: I hope the library buys *Out of the Dust* by Karen Hesse. I read a lot of books. Just last week I read four books from the Left Behind series and two by Frank Peretti. Those men sure are good writers. I want to read more by them.

3. **Don't contradict** yourself.
Wrong: The team sure could use me at first base. That's my strongest position unless I'm playing shortstop.

4. **Don't go on and on.** Keep it short and sweet.
Wrong: Putting a statue in the middle of our park was so stupid. I mean, who needs another statue? We already have four around town. Why do we need one more bronze hero up on a horse? Our town will get a bad reputation for all the statues we have cluttering up the landscape, and no one knows who those guys are anymore. There's one on the square, one at the post office, one at the school, one prancing on the hill, and now this one at the park. It's too much.

5. **Don't use "I think...,"** "I believe...," or "It is my opinion that...."
Wrong: It is my opinion that abortion is wrong.
Right: Abortion is wrong. **Right:** Abortion is harmful.

6. **Don't write without evidence**; don't exclude facts.
Wrong: Probably some other towns have recycling bins too. I can't think of any right now, but I'm sure there are some.

7. **Don't be vague.**
Wrong: I want to talk to you about a problem in our town. It has been here for a long time. Everyone is bothered by it. Can't you see how bad it has gotten in the past year? Isn't it awful? And now it's time to do something about it.

8. **Don't be illogical**; don't draw the wrong conclusions.
Wrong: No one waited on me, even though I was there first. I know it was because of my red hair and freckles. The employees must hate red hair and freckles. They waited on two blondes before they would even look at me.

9. **Don't use jargon** (lingo) or technical words that only a few know (unless you define them right away.)
Wrong: Be sure to attach the widget to the doohickey just under the spanner.

10. **Don't threaten** your audience or yell at them.
Wrong: If I were you, I would watch out from now on! The next time I go into your red-hair-and-freckles-hating store, I'm going to do some damage! You'll see. You can't ignore me and get away with it.

DO LIST

1. **Do treat** your reader intelligently.
Right: Teens, please show that you respect yourselves by dressing modestly.

2. **Do talk fairly** about the opposing view. Then prove it wrong.
Right: Many women say that abortion is an important part of women's rights. They want to be able to make decisions for themselves about their bodies. And that seems logical until you realize that there are a lot of little girls who will never have any rights because someone made the decision of death for them.

3. **Do quote** people, experts, or the Bible.
Right: I'm the right person for the first base position. Even Coach McGraw said last year, "If you want first base done right, rely on Pat. Nobody's better."

4. **Do be clear** about your topic.
Right: When I finished reading *Out of the Dust*, I knew other teens would like it. That's why I hope the library buys it.

5. **Do identify yourself** if it adds to your topic.
Right: I don't want the new highway to go through Vine Street. I should know. I've lived there all my life. **Right:** I am a frequent babysitter, so I know the importance of first aid training.

6. **Do define** your terms.
Right: Open your bumbershoot (umbrella) with care.

7. **Do know your audience.** Know their age, gender, interests, etc.
Wrong for a newspaper: Various personages subscribe to the fortuitous vicissitudes of existence. (This means that some people believe in chance, but it is too wordy for a newspaper, which is normally written for a 12-year-old reading level.)

Wrong: If you write a letter to the editor of your city's newspaper about how your church should have blue hymnals instead of red, you will be forgetting that most of the readers don't attend your church.

Right: When you write that article on friendship for *Brio* magazine (published by Focus on the Family), you will write it for Christian girls who are 12 to 16 years old.

Right: When you give your Christian testimony in church, you use words and phrases that everyone there understands. But when you give your testimony to a friend who is not a Christian and who hasn't ever been to church, you will use words that he understands. You will mean the same thing, but you will use different words.

Avoid everything on the **DON'T LIST**. Using anything from that list will only weaken your argument and make you look like you don't know what you're doing.

Use everything from the **DO LIST** that will help your paper. You will strengthen your argument and sound more intelligent.

Now it's your turn. Which items from the **DON'T LIST** were interesting or new to you? Write them below.

Which items from the **DO LIST** were interesting or new to you? Write them below.

Skill 10: The **Assignment**

CHOOSE **ONE**:

❏ Finish the original topic you chose on page 31 (in Skill 2).   Remember to **persuade** your reader. Word count: at least 200 words.

❏ Finish the letter to the librarian about the great/horrible video or book. When you finish this assignment, consider calling your local library to ask for the name of the library's purchaser. Then mail your letter to him or her. Word count: at least 200 words.

❏ Your choice. Choose a topic and use your new skills to **persuade** the reader to believe and behave a certain way. Word count: at least 200 words.

A suggested writing schedule:

Day 1   ► Brainstorm ideas.   Decide on your topic, three reasons, an order, and a purpose statement.

Days 2-3   ► Write the supporting statements for three separate paragraphs.

Day 4   ► Write the introduction and conclusion.

Day 5   ► Put the paragraphs in the right order. Proofread three separate times for mistakes. Make a neat copy.

Turn to page 238 and read **Mistake Medic.** Use it as your guide to proofread **everything you write.** Live with it. Eat with it. Breathe with it. It is your friend!

Persuasion: Cause and Effect

Skill 1: You **Push** me and I **Fall In!**

When you push your brother into the pool, he gets wet (and angry). When a friend gives you a gift, you smile and open the present. That's **cause and effect**—an action and a result. Let's set it up in a chart:

Cause (the action)	Effect (the result)
You push your brother into the pool.⟶	He gets wet and angry.
A friend gives you a gift. ⟶	You smile and open the present.

The *cause and effect* tool is great to use in a persuasive paper. It can be summed up very neatly by the following statements:

- Because of this event, many **good** things have happened.

OR

- Because of this event, many **bad** things have happened.

If you put it in terms of the pool incident, your cause and effect statement will look like this:

Because I pushed my brother into the pool, he got wet, he got angry, and he pushed me in.

Read this cause-and-effect statement for an invention:

Because of refrigeration, all these good things have happened: 1) People are healthier, 2) floral arrangements are available all year long, and 3) doctors and nurses can do their jobs better.

Now it's your turn. Think about an invention and write it in the space below. Decide whether this invention has been either helpful to the world or harmful. Then support your belief by writing all the **good** things that have happened because of that invention or all the **bad** things that have happened because of it.
Many inventions could easily go either way, so it is up to you to decide which way you want to prove—good or bad. It is also up to you to write strong points to support your belief and prove to the reader that the invention has been helpful or harmful.

Invention: _____

Circle which one you are going to prove: It has been good.   It has been bad.

List the things that have happened because of this invention (remember to choose between good **or** bad):

1.

2.

3.

4.

5.

6.

Skill 2: What's your **Order?**

You chose your invention and wrote six good things or six bad things that have happened because of the invention. Before you go any further, you will write a **purpose statement**.

Your *purpose statement* will not appear in your persuasive paper, but it will guide everything you write about the invention. Remember that a persuasive paper tries to convince the reader to **believe** and **behave** a certain way. For example, if you chose the telephone as your invention, you might use this as your purpose statement:

- I will convince the reader that the telephone has been a useful invention because of all the good things it helps us do.

In other words,

- Because the telephone was invented, all these good things have happened…

Then at the end of your paper, you will encourage your reader to use the telephone more.

Now it's your turn. In the space below, write your own purpose statement about the invention you chose on page 50 (in Skill 1).

I will convince the reader_____

_____

_____

Now choose your three best points from page 50 and circle their numbers. These are the points you will use for the body (middle part) of your paper. The next thing to do is to choose which order to put your points in. There are many good ways to do this. Read the four examples on the next page.

Importance	Importance	Chronological	Effect Size
Most important Next important Least important	Next important Least important Most important	Long ago Sometime later Most recent	Small Medium Large

To review examples of the first two boxes, turn back to page 34 and read the boxes there. Keep reading here to see examples of how to use the **chronological order** and the **effect size order**. Let's use the telephone as our cause-and-effect topic. In the reasons below, good things have happened because of the invention of the telephone:

Chronological Order

- **Long ago:** When the telephone was first invented in the late 1800s, it helped relatives stay in touch with each other.

- **Sometime later:** As more and more people had telephones installed in their homes and businesses, they were able to call the police, their doctors, or the fire station when there was trouble.

- **Most recent:** Today, we can dial 911 for instant help.

The *chronological order* begins with the telephone's usefulness when it was first invented. The next point was years later when more people and businesses had telephones. The last point is one helpful way we use the telephone today. Now watch what happens in the *effect size order* below:

Effect Size Order

- **Small:** I can use the telephone to call a friend and keep in touch.

- **Medium:** Our church uses a phone tree for changes in the schedule and for prayer requests.

- **Large:** The president can call another leader and arrange for a peace conference.

Notice that the first point touches only a few people. The next point mentions a larger group. The last point shows that the telephone is a good thing for huge groups of people from different countries. The good effect of the telephone grew from small to large by arranging the points in their order of size.

Now it's your turn again. Choose the order you would like to use and write your choice below: either of the *importance orders*, the *chronological order*, or the *effect size order*. Then rearrange the three points you circled on page 50 (from Skill 1) into your new order and write them by the numbers below.

ORDER CHOICE: _____

1.

2.

3.

Skill 3: A strong Body

As you have already learned in "Persuasion: The Basics," all your points go in the middle of your paper and are called the **body**. Each point (the good or bad thing) will get its own paragraph and need supporting statements.

To support each point or reason, you can use a variety of tools. Here are some suggestions:

- **Facts** that prove your point
- A **story** that relates to your point
- Logical **statements** that show the rightness of your point
- A small **quotation** to show that an expert agrees with you
- **Examples** that prove your point

Let's go back to the telephone. One point in favor of the telephone will become the **topic sentence** (the idea you write the whole paragraph about):

- Our church's telephone tree has helped us many times.

Below are examples of ways to use your tools when you write the supporting statements for your topic sentence. Notice that the topic sentences below are the same with each tool. This will give you an idea of how each tool works. You will use one of the tools or a combination of them in each paragraph. Some of them are very similar to each other. Don't sweat the differences—just write!

- **Facts:** Our church's phone tree has helped us many times. Last year our church used the phone tree fourteen times. We needed to pray for people twelve times. Twice there were blizzards, so we had to cancel our Wednesday night services. I'm glad we didn't get caught out in the storms!

- A **story:** Our church's phone tree has helped us many times. When Courtney Wilcox was in that car accident last month, our youth group found out about it right away from the phone tree and prayed for her. While she was getting her leg put in a cast in the emergency room, she remembered the phone tree and knew we were praying for her. Then she knew she would be OK.

- Logical **statements:** Our church's phone tree has helped us many times. We know who to pray for. We learn who needs help or a meal after surgery. Sometimes we even use the tree to cancel or postpone our meetings during bad weather because our church families live all over the county. I don't know how we could do all this without the telephone!

- A small **quotation:** Our church's phone tree has helped us many times. Our pastor recently told me this: "I am so grateful that each family is on the phone tree. Think about it. How else would we have known that Josh was hurt in the hurricane and needed our prayers? All the teens found out in time and prayed for him."

- **Examples:** Our church's phone tree has helped us many times. Emily used the phone tree when her mother was sick. Then we all prayed and brought over food. Joel used it during his mission trip to India. When he called with a prayer request, all of us teens knew right away what to pray about. And who can forget the year the tornado hit? Every family got the message from the phone tree and came to pray around the only thing left of our church building—the basement!

Now it's your turn. Choose one of the three points you wrote on page 53 (at the end of Skill 2). Use it as your topic sentence. Then finish the paragraph with supporting statements (*facts,* a *story, logical statements,* a *quotation,* or *examples*). The words *points* and *reasons* mean the same thing here.

TOPIC SENTENCE (why it's good/bad):

SUPPORTING STATEMENTS (the rest of the paragraph):

Skill 4: **Head** and **Feet**

This body needs a head and feet—a top and bottom. In other words, it's time to write an introductory paragraph and a concluding paragraph.

Your **introduction** is one paragraph long and will include what the invention is, who its inventor is, a *brief* history of it, and whether it has been a good or a bad thing. Your reader needs to know in the very first paragraph what your opinion of this invention is. From the very beginning, you will be persuading the reader to believe as you do about this invention.

When you have an interesting first sentence, people will want to keep reading. It can be a **statement, fact, quotation, question,** or **story**. Turn to page 21 to review each of these. No introduction should be without one.

Now it's your turn. Create your introductory paragraph below. Because this is a short exercise, you won't need to do the research about your invention. Don't forget to begin with a bang. When you have finished writing your introduction, read the next page.

INTRODUCTION:

Your **conclusion** is the last paragraph. It is your last chance to sway the reader to your way of thinking. It is also your chance to challenge your reader to behave a certain way. If you consider an invention to be bad, you might tell your reader to throw it away, change it, use it less, or make a better one. Challenge him to do something about it. The same tools you used in your introduction (an interesting **statement, fact, quotation, question,** or **story**) are useful here, too, along with a **call to action**.

Now it's your turn again. This is it! Make that last paragraph powerful. Use the space below.

CONCLUSION:

Skill 5: Pass the **Lemonade**, please

Below is an example of a cause-and-effect persuasive paper. It contains 291 words. Read it and answer the questions that follow it.

Brrr! It's Cold in Here!

Ice-cold sodas in the middle of a sizzling summer and fresh garden vegetables on the coldest winter days. What makes these possible? Your refrigerator.
Instead of storing food in a cold stream or an icebox, we use handy refrigerators. When Jacob Perkins built the first useful refrigeration machine in 1834, he had no idea all the wonderful ways it would be used.

Did you know that doctors and nurses around the world rely on refrigerators? Refrigerators keep blood and plasma safe for people who need transfusions. Many medicines can be refrigerated and shipped all over the world. Even in countries where electricity is available only in the cities, refrigerators operated by batteries or propane contain precious immunizations that will prevent diseases. But doctors and nurses aren't the only ones who benefit from refrigeration.

Thanks to refrigerators, many people are living healthier lifestyles. We don't have to rely only on the foods that are in season, but we can eat a variety of meats, fruits, vegetables, and dairy products no matter what season it is. Because refrigeration controls bacteria that produce diseases, we now have fewer food-related illnesses. This is true in both our homes and our businesses.

The refrigerator is not only practical but also makes a beautiful product available to everyone. Almost every grocery store refrigerates this product. Hospitals refrigerate them too. Even whole stores revolve around them. What are they? Flowers. Refrigeration has made it possible for anyone to enjoy fresh, colorful flowers and floral arrangements all year long.

I don't think Mr. Perkins knew just how helpful his invention would turn out to be. The world is a safer, healthier, more beautiful place because of his refrigerator. Now, would you like a glass of cold lemonade with me?

Now it's your turn.   Answer the questions below and on the next page.

1. Did the first sentence interest you? (It isn't a complete sentence, but work with me here.)

2. How did the writer let you know that the refrigerator is a good invention without saying, "The refrigerator is good"?

3. Why was the last sentence a good one to end with?

4. What were the writer's three reasons why the refrigerator is good? In other words, what has its effect been on people and the world?

❑

❑

❑

5. Underline the order the writer used for the reasons: one of the importance orders, chronological order, or effect size order.

6. Based on your knowledge of cause and effect, what grade would you give this student?

⇨   The interesting thing about the cause-and-effect tool is that you can use it for essays in many different school subjects. In subjects other than persuasion, you will often include both the good and the bad results. Read the examples below:

- **Science:** Because people believed Charles Darwin in his book *On the Origin of Species,* these bad things have happened… (The rest of your paper will talk about three or four bad things.)

- **Science:** Because the volcano Mount St. Helens blew up, all these negative changes happened in the ecological systems nearby…

- **History:** Because of the Boston Tea Party, all these good **and** bad things happened to the American colonists…

- **History:** Because both America and Germany learned to use airplanes in World War II, all these good **and** bad things happened…

- **Literature:** Because Huckleberry Finn took the runaway slave, Jim, with him on his raft, all these good **and** bad things happened to Huck…

Now turn the page.

Your purpose statement for, say, Mount St. Helens would be something like this:

- I am going to show that because Mount St. Helens exploded, many negative things happened to the ecology in the surrounding area.

Your purpose statement for writing about Huck and Jim would look something like this:

- I am going to show that because Huck took the slave, Jim, with him on the raft, many negative and positive things happened to Huck.

Your purpose statement will not appear in your paper, but it will guide your thinking as you research and write.

Remember that in a <u>persuasive paper,</u> you have to convince your reader that you are right, so you have to **choose** whether the event was a good thing or a bad thing. You can't be wishy-washy and say it was both!

Sometimes your teacher wants to see that you understand all the positive and negative effects of a scientific or historical event.

However, if you are writing an essay for <u>another school subject</u> and you want to show *all* the effects—both good and bad—make a "good" list and a "bad" list before you begin to write. Then you will write about both the good and the bad effects of the event.

Skill 6: The **Assignment**

CHOOSE **ONE**:

☐ Finish the cause-and-effect persuasive paper you have already begun. Put the paragraphs in the right order. Word count: at least 250 words.

☐ Choose some other invention. Determine whether you want to show its good effects **or** bad effects on people. Write your persuasive paper about it. Word count: at least 250 words.

☐ Your choice. Choose another cause-and-effect topic and write a persuasive paper on all the good things **or** bad things that have happened because of it (a war, a scientific discovery, a decision by a king, the last thing you bought, etc.). Word count: at least 250 words.

A suggested writing schedule:

Day 1   ► Brainstorm. Decide on your invention/topic. Decide whether it is good or bad. List three reasons.

Days 2-3   ► Write the supporting statements for your reasons in three separate paragraphs.

Day 4   ► Research your invention/topic and write a brief history of it. When you have finished with this step, you may want to change some of your reasons to include the new information.

Day 5   ► Write the introduction and conclusion.

Day 6   ► Put the paragraphs in the right order. Proofread three separate times for mistakes. Make a neat copy.

Remember to use the **Mistake Medic** on page 238 in **YOUR LOCKER**!

Exposition: The Basics

Skill 1: **What?**

Exposition is a big word with an easy explanation: writing to **explain** or **teach** something, inspire, or even entertain. It is nonfiction—dealing with facts. It's that simple. Take a look at the list below. These are examples of *expository writing*. It's everywhere:

- Encyclopedia entries
- Newspaper articles
- Magazine articles
- Handbooks, instructions and instruction manuals
- Books on pets, countries, the solar system, etc.
- Essays by famous authors in literature books
- Biographies and autobiographies
- Other nonfiction books (reference books, textbooks, cookbooks, etc.)

Every report or essay you've ever written is exposition.

Check your science and history books. They're exposition. The authors are not making up stories (fiction); they are teaching you facts or explaining things.

Look up the word *calendar* in any encyclopedia, and you will see that the entry is teaching you about calendars.

Learn about the water supply in India from *National Geographic* or persecution in Indonesia from *The Voice of the Martyrs* magazine.

Buy a sewing pattern, and it will explain how to make a beach tote out of a beach towel and ribbons.

Read Hans Christian Andersen's autobiography. Even that is exposition—the true story about his life.

Now it's your turn. This will reveal to you the hidden riches of expository writing. Get an encyclopedia and look up a word of your choice. If you don't have an encyclopedia handy, get a book about deserts, lizards, robots, horses, or something that interests you.

Read one good-sized paragraph from the encyclopedia or the reference book. In the space below, write the facts from the paragraph. Your facts do not have to be in complete sentences.

FACTS:

When you finish writing the facts, close the book. Using only the notes you just took, rewrite the paragraph in your own words. Use the space below and on the next page.

Go back and reread the paragraph from your book. How close were you to the original text?

Try this exercise often. It is short, and it will teach you amazing things about writing.

Reconstructing someone else's writing is an *extremely* useful tool. Benjamin Franklin reconstructed other authors' essays when he wanted to learn how to write essays better. You can too. Putting something into your own words is called **paraphrasing**, and you will use it every time you take notes.

Skill 2: Put me back **Together!**

Now it's your turn. Get a pair of scissors and look at the next page. Those sentences used to be in an orderly paragraph, but now they are out of order. Cut them apart and lay them on your desk. It is your job to put them back together as close to the original paragraph as you can.

First, find the topic sentence (what the paragraph is about). Then fill in the rest. When you have your sentences in the order you think they should be, check with your teacher to see how close you came to the original.

Cut out the sentences and try to assemble them in their original order. This is one paragraph from a **report** on the history of the calendar.

Later, people paid attention to the moon and its phases (new moon, full moon, etc.).

They knew that things began to grow again at the same time every year.

That time became known as a *month*, named for the moon.

At first, people kept track of the year by the seasons.

The time it takes for the moon to go through all its phases is about 29½ days.

The phases were named for the different shapes the moon seems to have.

The calendar we use today hasn't always been around.

Today we call that season *spring*.

Skill 3: From **Broad** to **Narrow**

When your teacher gives you an assignment, all you have to do is brainstorm ideas, organize your thoughts, do a little research, and write your report or essay.

But what if your teacher gives you a broad topic or lets you choose your own topic? What do you do then?

If your assignment is to write a report about fire, you have a problem. The topic is too broad. It is too big. You need to narrow it down. Think of all the different smaller topics within the topic of fire. Here are some possibilities for narrower topics about fire:

- How man has used fire through the years
- How fire actually burns (the chemical process)
- How helpful fire can be
- How harmful fire can be
- How firemen put out fires
- How a fire affects a forest and how the forest recovers

These are just a few narrowed-down ideas you could use for your report on fire. Can you think of any more?

Now it's your turn. Your topic is horses. Practice narrowing down this broad topic. The first two are done for you. Think of four more. Then turn the page.

1. How man has used horses through the years

2. The difference between horses and donkeys

3.

4.

5.

6.

Here's another broad topic: the sun. Write down four narrower topics that have something to do with the sun—something you could do a report on.

1.

2.

3.

4.

Was it hard? Easy? Fun? Don't stop now! Here's the last topic that is too broad: Italy. Narrow it down. List some topics within the Italy topic that you could write about.

1.

2.

3.

4.

▷ It is possible to narrow down your topic too much. If you can't find enough information when you do your research, consider doing a report on some other part of your topic. Or simply make your narrowed-down topic a little bigger.

As an example, instead of writing about kookaburras (for which it might be difficult to find information), you may need to write about *many* birds from Australia.

Skill 4: What's the **Big Idea?**

Before you can organize your thoughts, you have to know the direction you are taking with your report or essay. You've practiced narrowing down a topic. Now you have to give your topic a direction.

If your topic is the nation Greece, and you narrow it down to Greek mythology, think about what you want to say about Greek mythology. You can't write everything about Greek mythology. It would take years!

- Do you want to show how we got some of our English words (like *arachnid*, *echo*, and *narcissus*) from the ancient myths?
- Do you want to compile some of the stories and show their history and the major characters?
- Do you want to explain that many of the Greek gods and goddesses morphed into the Roman ones when the Romans came into power?
- Do you want to show that the old gods the Greeks believed in are nowhere near as loving and just as our holy God?

Think about it. What do you want your paper to say? On a piece of paper, you will write this: "In my paper, I want to say <u>this</u> about Greek mythology...." Then you will fill in what you want to say. This is for your own use. It is your purpose statement. Your main idea, however, will appear in your paper. If you choose how we got many English words from the ancient myths, your **main idea** or **thesis statement** might look like this:

- It is surprising how many of our words come from Greek mythology.

If you choose to compare the old Greek gods and goddesses with the one true God, your **main idea** or **thesis statement** might look like this:

- Those selfish, jealous, mean gods and goddesses of ancient Greece were not at all like the one true God.

Your *main idea* (*thesis statement*) will be a complete sentence and will state the direction your report or essay is taking. It should say something interesting about your narrowed-down topic. Most of the time, your main idea will be the last sentence in your introductory paragraph. It will guide everything you write in your report or essay, and it will tell your reader what to expect.

> Your thesis statement is the big idea that will tie the whole paper together. It is the direction you are taking your topic.

Now it's your turn. Below are sample topics. Narrow down the topics. Then write a main idea about what you want to say about the topic. You can do this whether the topic is a person, an event, or a thing. Look at the example and fill in the spaces below.

<u>EXAMPLE</u>

Topic: the current president/leader
Narrowed down: his growing up years
Main idea (thesis statement): The difficulties this man overcame as a youth helped him to become a better leader.

<u>YOUR TURN</u>

Topic: Egypt

Narrowed down:

Main idea (thesis statement):

Try it one more time:

Topic: the solar system

Narrowed down:

Main idea (thesis statement):

> At first, you might not be able to come up with a direction for your report. That is perfectly OK. Often, you will develop your main idea *as you read your books*. Something you read there may be very interesting to you, and you will base your whole report on that. Or you will understand the subject better and be able to organize your thoughts around a main idea/thesis statement.

Skill 5: But I **Meant...**

Mrs. Tyler yelled up the stairs.
"You boys had better make that bedroom shine, or I won't take you with me to Burger Barn!"
"What did she say?" Jared asked while a CD blared. "I couldn't hear her."
"She said we have to clean our room if we want to eat out tonight," said Jamaal.

Look at what Mrs. Tyler told her sons. Then read what Jamaal told his brother. The two sentences are not the same, but they *mean* the same thing.

When you read words and write down their *meaning* instead of their exact words, you are **paraphrasing**. This is an essential skill to have as you take notes. Why? If you write down someone else's exact words and use them in your report (without giving them the credit for the words), you are plagiarizing.

Is that bad? Yes, it is illegal. And just plain lazy.

Jamaal *paraphrased* his mother's words by telling Jared their mother's meaning. And that is what you will do when you take notes.

Now it's your turn. You are going to practice paraphrasing by using the first two paragraphs of Lincoln's Gettysburg Address, delivered November 19, 1863. The two paragraphs have 102 words in them, so this will be short. Don't go word by word. Do a phrase or a sentence at a time. Read a whole sentence first to understand it. Then write down what the sentence means. Use a separate piece of paper.

If you want more practice in paraphrasing, get your Bible and turn to Matthew 6:9-13. You will be paraphrasing the Lord's Prayer.

Four score and seven years ago our fathers brought forth on this continent a new nation, conceived in Liberty and dedicated to the proposition that all men are created equal.

Now we are engaged in a great civil war, testing whether that nation, or any nation so conceived and so dedicated, can long endure. We are met on a great battlefield of that war. We have come to dedicate a portion of that field as a final resting place for those who here gave their lives that that nation might live. It is altogether fitting and proper that we should do this.

Skill 6: Gone **Fishing!**

After you've narrowed down your topic and have the main idea/thesis statement for your report or essay, what do you do next?

You go fishing. You begin your fishing by going to the library and catching some books to take home. Then you spread a large net and capture many facts from those books.

Read this list of information you might look for if your report is on an animal:

- what the animal looks like (if it is a strange animal)
- where it lives (the country and its natural habitat)
- what it eats
- what its social habits are (family life, community life)
- how long it lives
- who its enemies are, etc.

If you are writing a report on a country, you might look for these facts:

- where it is
- some of its history
- what its flag looks like
- what the language is
- what the religion is
- what its people are like
- what they wear
- imports and exports
- other natural resources
- its government
- climate

As you haul in the facts, you will put them down on notebook paper.

Buy an 8½" x 11" notebook or put 8½" x 11" paper into a three-ring binder. Now you are ready to begin.

On the last page in your notebook, record all the bibliography information from all of your sources. In front of each source, put a letter (A, B, C, D, etc.). You will use these letters when you take your notes. You can find a format for your sources in any grammar book, or you may use the format on the next page, approved by *The Chicago Manual of Style*, 15th edition.

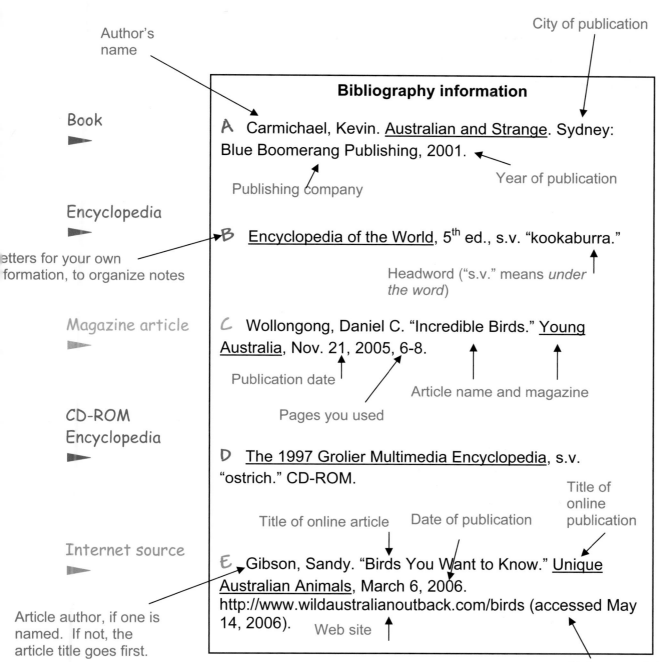

Bibliography information

Author's name

City of publication

Book ▶

A Carmichael, Kevin. <u>Australian and Strange</u>. Sydney: Blue Boomerang Publishing, 2001.

Publishing company

Year of publication

Encyclopedia ▶

Letters for your own information, to organize notes

B <u>Encyclopedia of the World</u>, 5th ed., s.v. "kookaburra."

Headword ("s.v." means *under the word*)

Magazine article ▶

C Wollongong, Daniel C. "Incredible Birds." <u>Young Australia</u>, Nov. 21, 2005, 6-8.

Publication date

Pages you used

Article name and magazine

CD-ROM Encyclopedia ▶

D <u>The 1997 Grolier Multimedia Encyclopedia</u>, s.v. "ostrich." CD-ROM.

Title of online publication

Title of online article

Date of publication

Internet source ▶

Article author, if one is named. If not, the article title goes first.

E Gibson, Sandy. "Birds You Want to Know." <u>Unique Australian Animals</u>, March 6, 2006. http://www.wildaustralianoutback.com/birds (accessed May 14, 2006).

Web site

Date you printed it from the Web site

Underlined titles in your notes should be italicized on a computer. Remember to remove the underline. However, if you are writing your report by hand, underline the book and magazine titles.

Your computer will try to keep the Web address together. If there is no space on one line, it will put it on the next line. If there is enough space, try to put it just after the date of publication.

When you make your bibliography page for your report, put each entry in order alphabetically, using authors' last names. Where there is no author (as in some Internet entries), use the first word of the magazine article's title.

Below is an example of what your bibliography would look like at the end of your report if you were to use the sources on the previous page (which are all fake except for the CD-ROM entry).

Bibliography

Carmichael, Kevin. *Australian and Strange*. Sydney: Blue Boomerang
     Publishing, 2001.

Gibson, Sandy. "Birds You Want to Know." *Unique Australian Animals*,
     March 6, 2006. http://www.wildaustralianoutback.com/birds
     (accessed May 14, 2006).

Wollongong, Daniel C. "Incredible Birds." *Young Australia*, Nov. 21,
     2005, 6-8.

Sometimes you may use Works Cited at the top of the page instead of Bibliography. Check with your teacher to see which to use.

You will be clever enough to notice some differences between the informal bibliography information on the previous page and the bibliography above:

- First, the bibliography is alphabetical by author (or title of article if no author is listed).
- Second, the letters before each entry have been removed. They were only for your benefit as you kept track of your notes.
- Third, the encyclopedia entries are missing. Encyclopedias are often not listed in a *Chicago*-style bibliography at the end of your paper. Check with your teacher to see if you should include these.
- Last, each entry uses a hanging indentation. In other words, each entry begins on the far left side of the page, but the second and third lines begin a few spaces in. Learn how to do this on your computer.

Check your grammar book to learn how to cite any sources that are not in the examples on pages 75 and 76 (videos, books by two authors, etc.).

Now it's your turn. Below are the publishing facts from a real book. Rearrange them below as they would appear in a bibliography or works cited page. Include the correct punctuation marks and the hanging indentation.

The Great Dinosaur Mystery and the Bible
1987
Master Books
San Diego
Paul S. Taylor

_____

_____

_____

Now it's your turn again. Below are the publishing facts from a real Internet source. Rearrange them below as they would appear in a bibliography or works-cited page. Use the correct punctuation marks and the hanging indentation.

Feb. 1987
Paul Humber
"The Ascent of Racism"
http://www.icr.org/pubs/imp/imp-164.htm
June 14, 2005
Impact

_____

_____

_____

Skill 7: Spreading the Net

Taking notes is easy. The notebook method is so easy that many journalists do it a similar way.

At the top of each page, put the topic heading. In fact, put the topic heading on two pages in case you find a lot of information on that topic. But don't write on the backs of the pages.

The topic for this sample report below is birds of Australia.

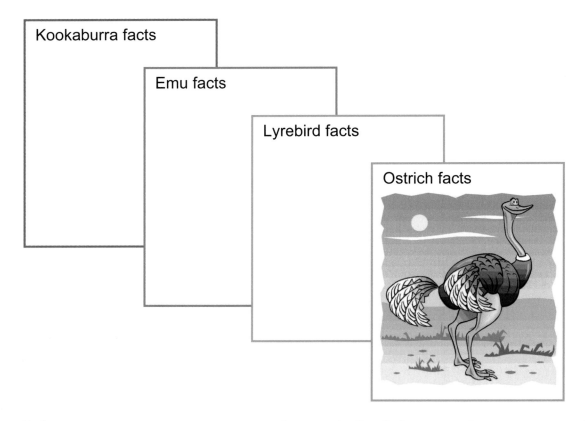

Make sure to put your source code—an A, B, C, D, etc.—from your notebook bibliography page next to each fact in your notes (see the next page). Also include the page number of the book or magazine. That way you can look up something later that seems confusing, or you can refer back to that page for more information.

If your source is from the Internet, print the pages you read there and keep them. Many times the information you read today won't be there tomorrow; it is a good thing to have proof of your facts.

Because you write your facts only on the fronts of the pages, you will find your facts quickly and easily when it comes time to write your report.

Read the sample notes on the next page.

Emu facts

on Australia's coat of arms – A, p. 14

People used to treat them as enemies because there were so many of them. They ate the cattle's grass and broke down fences. – A, p. 15

Adults are 5 feet tall. – C, p. 6

brown and gray feathers – C, p. 6

lays 10-12 dark green eggs almost 5" long – E

The male sits on the nest and drives the female away. – E

doesn't fly – B

They can run fast and swim. - B

Each source is noted by an A, B, C, etc., next to the fact. This keeps things straight if you need to go back and check something later. Review page 75 (Skill 6) to see which sources correspond with which letters. Notice that some of the above notes also contain page numbers. Also, the notes are paraphrased from the original sources.

The best way to get ideas for what to write is to read the books and other sources. They are already written in logical paragraphs and chapters. This will help you organize your notes and your final report.

Now it's your turn. On the next page are some jumbled-up facts about Panama that belong under the headings "Food," "Geography," and "People." Get three sheets of notebook paper and put one heading at the top of each sheet. Then transfer each fact to the correct sheet, according to its topic. Some of the facts are complete sentences; some are not. That's OK.

Panamanian staples: rice, corn, legumes and beans, yams, cassava (an edible root), plantains (a kind of banana)

a "melting pot" of ethnic cultures   includes more than 1,500 islands

heavy rainfall, tropical   American Indians

The Pacific and Caribbean coasts are at sea level.   more than 3 million people

sancocho—rich, hearty soup made with chicken and vegetables

Mountains run through the middle of Panama like a spine.

Kuna Indians in the San Blas Islands   Pacific coasts have mudflats at low tide.

descendants of black slaves (brought to dive for pearls years ago)

longest mountain range called the Cordillera Central

land bridge between Central and South America   Panama 480 miles long

30 to 75 miles wide   descendants of Spanish from the 1500s to the 1800s

tamales—of cornmeal dough, stuffed with chicken, pork, or vegetables, wrapped in banana leaves and boiled

descendants of Chinese railroad workers   country shaped like an "S" lying down

arroz con guando—rice and beans cooked in coconut milk

Mestizos, blend of American Indians and Spanish, most of them living in poverty

long, narrow isthmus called the Isthmus of Panama

hojaldras—flat dough fried, sometimes with sprinkled sugar

highest elevation—Barú Volcano at 11,401 feet   lots of seafood

Many blacks from the West Indies, Jamaica, or Barbados worked on the canal in early 1900s.

separates Pacific Ocean from the Caribbean Sea and on to the Atlantic Ocean

many other European, East Asian, and Middle Eastern countries represented in the population

Skill 8: **Organize** the **Chaos**, part I

After you gather your notes, you are going to have to stop and think before you write. What are the main points you want to include? What supporting facts will help? In what order will you put everything?

There are many good ways to organize your information. Today you'll look at two—the outline method and the list method. In Skill 9, you'll look at two more. Any will get the job done. You get to choose which one will help you the most.

Look at the silly examples below and think about which method of organizing you would rather use. The report is about a fictitious disease.

Outline for heebie-jeebie disease

I. Introductory paragraph
    A. Clever story
    B. Thesis statement (main idea)
II. Facts about the disease
    A. How you can get it
        1. People sneezing on you
        2. People yelling at you
    B. Symptoms
        1. Purple dots in the shape of Texas
        2. Headaches when you have to clean your room
III. History of the disease
    A. The discoverer
    B. What people thought it was before he discovered it
IV. How to cure it
    A. Avoid all people
    B. Wear rubber gloves to bed
    C. Don't clean your room
V. Concluding paragraph
    A. Refer back to the clever story
    B. State my desire that the reader doesn't get this dreaded disease

---

List for heebie-jeebie disease

1. Introduction with story and thesis statement (main idea)
2. How people can get it
3. Symptoms of it
4. The discoverer
5. What people thought it was before that and how they treated it
6. The cure
7. Conclusion with something to tie in to the story in paragraph one

This list is smaller than the outline, but yours doesn't have to be. You can put as much on your list as you want to. By keeping it short, you will have to refer to your notes to fill in the extras. *Each Roman numeral of the outline is a new paragraph.*   Much of the organizing is already done when you write your outline. Notice that the thesis statement goes at the end of your introductory paragraph.

Now it's your turn.   Which method of organizing did you like best?   Mark which method you prefer and state why.

☐ The outline

☐ The list

Why:

Now it's your turn again. Pretend you have to write a report on the benefits of bicycle riding. Also pretend you have already done the research. In order to do this exercise, on a separate piece of paper brainstorm your ideas on the benefits of bike riding. Then organize your thoughts using the **outline** or the **list**, using only three or four of the benefits you brainstormed. (Each benefit will become a separate paragraph in the body of your imaginary report.) Write a detailed outline or a detailed list for your bicycle topic. Use the space below.

Skill 9: **Organize** the **Chaos**, part II

As promised, you will learn two other methods of how to organize your facts before you write. In Skill 8, you learned the outline and list methods. Today you will explore the **cluster method** and the **Greek temple method**. Remember that the *cluster method* looks like a solar system. The main idea/thesis statement or your topic is the sun in the middle, and all the points are the planets. Items related to the points are like moons to the planets.

Below you will find a topic, the thesis statement, and an organized cluster of facts. The colors help keep the "sun" and "planets" organized. The numbers indicate paragraph order. Each planet will become a separate paragraph in the report. Read the "solar system" below and then turn the page:

Topic: the heebie-jeebie disease
Main idea (thesis statement): I had caught the famous heebie-jeebie disease.

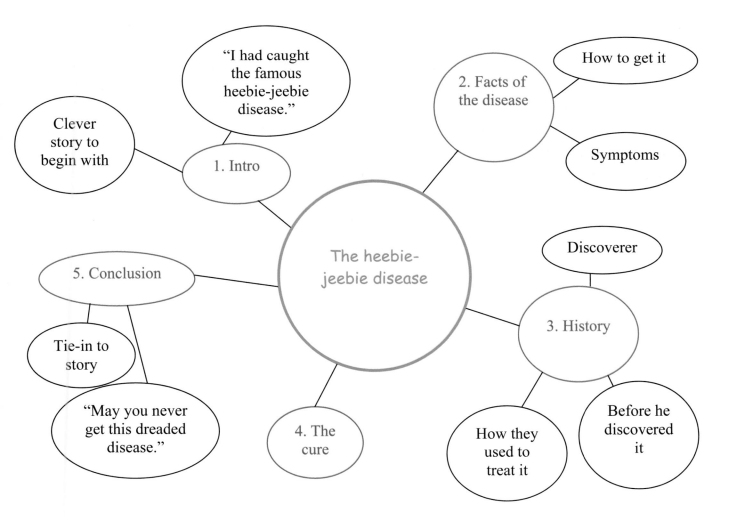

The second method you'll learn today uses a Greek temple—well, the sketch of a Greek temple. Here's an illustration you easily will remember from your history books. Believe it or not, you can use it to organize your thoughts. Each column (point) becomes a separate paragraph in the body of your report. Look at this example:

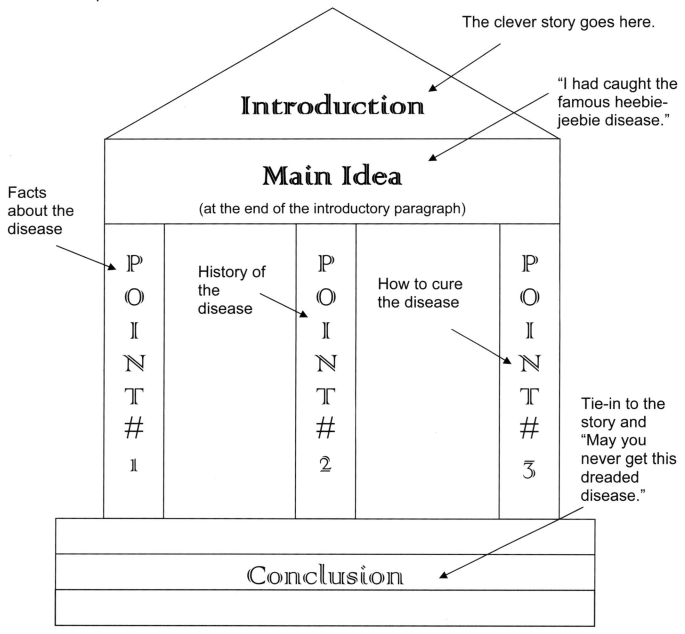

Now it's your turn. Use your notes on the benefits of bicycle riding. Decide on a main idea/thesis statement. Now organize it all into a cluster or a Greek temple to organize your thoughts and decide on paragraphs for your imaginary report. Use a separate piece of paper.

Skill 10: The **Spice** of **Life**

At some point in this process, you have to begin to write. Yes, you do. Putting words down on paper can be the most frustrating part of writing.

Don't begin at the beginning if you don't want to! You may write the body first, and you may write the introduction and the conclusion last if you like. Remember to turn off your internal editor that tells you how stupid your first sentence is. You can always go back and fix things later!

If you were to gather the reports of three friends and read them, you would know which friend wrote which report, even if the names were left off the papers. How? By the way they use their words and sentences, and by the way they say things on paper. Your own style is just as distinctive. You have a certain way, a certain pattern, of writing.

Here are two things to keep in mind when you write anything:

- Vary your sentence length.

- Vary your sentence structure.

Sentence length: A report can get boring if each sentence is the same length. Mix in some short sentences with the longer ones. As a general rule, try to keep your sentences no longer than 20 words. This will help your reader understand what you write.

Sentence structure: Writing the same kind of sentence (simple declarative) over and over gets monotonous to write and to read. Use a variety of sentence structures to guarantee an interesting paper. Try using compound sentences (combining two complete sentences with an *and, but, or*, etc.). Once in a while, consider an introductory phrase. Do you ever sprinkle in a question to vary your sentence structure?

Now it's your turn. Use only the <u>first three paragraphs</u> on this page.
1. **Count the words in each sentence** in the first three paragraphs on this page. Write the number in the left margin next to each sentence. Check me! Did I vary the length of my sentences?
2. **Label the sentences.** Use the right margin. Write CS for compound sentence, D for declarative, I for interrogatory (question), IMP for imperative, SS for compound subject, VV for compound verb, IP for any sentence with an introductory phrase, and F for fragment. Some sentences may have more than one label.

Skill 11: A hidden **Treasure**

Hidden inside almost every paragraph is a small treasure. It is called a **topic sentence**. The *topic sentence* tells you what the whole paragraph is about. Read the following paragraph and underline the topic sentence:

> Dogs hold many jobs. With a dog on the job, you, your family, and your property are safe. Trained to herd sheep, cattle, and even fish, as the Portuguese water dog is, dogs lighten the workloads of their owners. Countless lives are saved because dogs find explosives, illegal drugs, and people who are lost.

Which sentence did you underline? If you underlined the first one, you are correct. The first sentence of that paragraph is the topic sentence. All the other stuff in the paragraph supports or proves the topic sentence.

Here's another paragraph. Read it through and underline the topic sentence:

> One day, Benjamin Franklin saw a field where some spots of grass were greener than others. He decided to figure out why the grass was so green in those spots. He finally realized that earlier, someone had outlined letters on the field with white gypsum, much as we do for football games. Many people didn't believe that this was what made the grass greener; no artificial fertilizers were known at that time. But he was always making new discoveries.

How did you do? Which sentence did you underline? In this case, the topic sentence is the last sentence in that paragraph. Everything else in the paragraph supports, proves, and builds the topic sentence.

Here's one more. Read the paragraph below and underline the topic sentence:

> As a child by his mother's knee, young Robert E. Lee learned immediate obedience. His father died when he was six, so most of his training came from his mother. Of all the things he did, one of the most caring and inspiring was that when school let out every day, instead of playing with his friends, he went home to get his mother's carriage ready. When he had it ready, he would bring his mother out and take her around town.

OK. Which sentence is the topic sentence? Which one did you underline?

I have to apologize to you now because there is no topic sentence! Believe it or not, some topic sentences are **implied**. That means you can understand what the whole paragraph is about without one particular sentence to tell you what the topic is. So, what is the *implied* topic sentence for the paragraph about Robert E. Lee? Here are two possibilities:

- When he was young, he was kind.
- This paragraph is about what Robert E. Lee was like as a boy.

Because those are *so* obvious, the writer didn't need to put either sentence in the paragraph. But he kept the whole paragraph aimed at that invisible topic sentence anyway. Implied topic sentences are best used by more experienced writers. They are included here because you often find them in textbooks or encyclopedias.

Open any of your textbooks and read a paragraph at random. You will notice that most of the paragraphs don't have a topic sentence. They have implied topic sentences in each paragraph. The paragraph may be about the Spanish years of Puerto Rican history or about chlorophyll's job in photosynthesis, but it will be very easy to figure out what the topic of that paragraph is.

Now it's your turn. Below is a paragraph written about men and dinosaurs. It is missing its topic sentence. Read it and write a good topic sentence for its first sentence. Then go to the next page.

God created dinosaurs and man on the same day. There are even a few places on earth where fossils of dinosaur and human footprints are close together in the same layer of rock. One of these places is in Glen Rose, Texas, in a creek bed. Some painted pictures of dinosaurs have been found on the walls of caves of prehistoric Indians in America's Southwest. How could those men and women have painted such pictures without having seen a real dinosaur?

Write your topic sentence: _____

_____

_____

Here's another paragraph. It's about a form of transportation in Colonial American times. Read it and create a topic sentence. Then decide where to put it in the paragraph—at the beginning or the end.

Logs were laid down across the road, side by side in the mud and then packed with dirt. This helped a little on the muddy sections of the dirt roads, but it created other problems. As you can guess by its name, corduroy, which is also the name of a very bumpy fabric, it made the roads extremely uncomfortable, jolting travelers in carriages and making horses go lame.

Write your topic sentence: _____

_____

_____

Where does it best fit? ☐ the first sentence in the paragraph
                        ☐ the last sentence in the paragraph

Skill 12: Getting from **Here** to **There**

There is a trick you can use to get from one paragraph to the next. The trick is called a **transition sentence.** It can be the last sentence of a paragraph or the first sentence of the next paragraph. Wherever you put it, its job is to lead your reader smoothly to the next idea.

Read the report below, written by a boy in the sixth grade. It contains 249 words. Pay attention to his *transition sentences.* They lead you from one idea to the next, like guides on a tour. <u>Underline</u> his transition sentences. The first one is done for you.

Remembered Forever

The Flying Tigers were a group of American men who were very brave fighter pilots. They had to be made up of volunteers because the U.S.A. hadn't yet declared war on Japan. The volunteers were sent to China, secretly posing as engineers or ranchers. <u>When they arrived in China, they met their new commander.</u>

Claire Lee Chennault was a strong, sturdy, and stubborn man, but he also was kind and the creator of the Flying Tigers. He taught pilots to use and maneuver the P-40 (Tomahawk). Quickly he turned amateurs into aces. Tex Hill was one of them.

David "Tex" Lee Hill was a quick learner and an excellent flyer. Tex was from Texas. He was a fighter pilot in the Navy before going to China. He became a major and was placed in charge of his own fort. He performed acts of kindness that made his men love him. For example, he stopped the Japanese before they were off the ground so his men could get some rest. Although he was such a surprisingly first-rate pilot, there were still many other great pilots.

Bob Neale and Ed Rector were a couple of the many great fighter pilots in the war in China. Our bombers ended up smashingly knocking Japan out of the war in the skies.

The Flying Tigers ended up losing only 468 planes while destroying three thousand. Because China was being attacked by Japan, too, the Flying Tigers will be remembered by the Chinese people forever.

Now read the next page.

Now it's your turn. Read the two paragraphs below. They are about some of John Cabot's explorations and discoveries along the eastern coast of North America around the year 1500. Write a transition sentence in the blank to link the first paragraph with the next one. It will be the first sentence of the second paragraph.

From Labrador, Cabot sailed along the coast of North America until he nearly reached the peninsula of Florida. Once, he tried to form a colony. But the soil was barren, the men became discouraged, and the colony was given up.

_____

_____

_____

_____

In fact, Cabot called the country the "Land of the Codfish" because the seas contained such quantities of cod. The bears of the country were almost harmless, he said, since they could obtain such an abundance of food. They were accustomed to swim out into the water and catch the fish in their claws. Terrible struggles would take place as the fish, which were large and strong, tried to get away. The bears usually came off victors and would swim with their prey to the shore where they would eat it at their leisure.[1]

Now it's your turn again. On the next page are two more paragraphs about Cabot from the same book. The transition sentence between the two paragraphs is missing. Write it on the blanks. It will be the last sentence in the first paragraph this time.

---

[1] William Mowry and Arthur Mowry, *First Steps in the History of Our Country* (New York: Silver, Burdett and Company, 1907), 33-34.

After this second voyage, no trace of Cabot can be found. Whether he died on the return trip or soon after his arrival in England is not known.

_____

_____

_____

_____

The reason is that, because of these two voyages of John Cabot, England laid claim to the whole Atlantic coast from Labrador to Florida. Because she laid claim to it, she sent out colonists to take possession. And because she sent colonists, the people of the United States speak the English language. Had it not been for John Cabot, the inhabitants of this part of America might now have for their native tongue the Spanish language, as do the people of Mexico and most of the nations of South America.

When you have finished writing your two separate transition sentences, ask your teacher to show you the original ones.

Skill 13: You may **Quote** me!

There may come a time in a report when you want to quote someone. The person's words will be just right for your topic, and you won't want to paraphrase them. Basically, there are three things you need to include if you are quoting from a book or a magazine: 1) the author's name, 2) the title of the book or magazine article, and 3) the page the quotation is on.

Putting this information in parentheses is called *parenthetical notation.*

Below are many correct ways to quote from a book or magazine in your report. You will notice that all the facts are the same in all the examples (the author, book or magazine article title, page number, and quotation):

Book title italicized ↓   Quotation ↓

- According to *Clean that Room*, "Children would rather hide their junk than organize their clutter" (Spratt 5).

Author ↑   ↑ Page number

- Jack Spratt says, "Children would rather hide their junk than organize their clutter" (*Clean that Room* 5).

- Jack Spratt writes that "children would rather hide their junk than organize their clutter" (*Clean that Room* 5).

- Jack Spratt, author of *Clean that Room*, makes this astounding remark: "Children would rather hide their junk than organize their clutter" (5).

- "Children would rather hide their junk than organize their clutter," says Jack Spratt, author of *Clean that Room* (5).

- As Jack Spratt points out, "Children would rather hide their junk than organize their clutter" ("Clean that Room" 5).

↑_____ Title of magazine article in quotation marks

Obviously, there are many right ways to quote someone in your report. Use the formats above or ask your teacher for others. The important thing is to tell your reader where you got your information. That's called *citing your sources*.

Citing an Internet source is easy. You may use either of these formats:

- According to www.cleanthatroom.org, "Children would rather hide their junk than organize their clutter."

- "Children would rather hide their junk than organize their clutter," according to www.cleanthatroom.org.

Remember to turn off your hyperlink by right-clicking on the address and left-clicking on "Hyperlink" and "Remove Hyperlink."

Internet sites often do not include an author's name. However, if one is included, be polite and include it in your quotation information:

- According to Jack Spratt at www.cleanthatroom.org, "Children would rather hide their junk than organize their clutter."

When you use a quotation in your report, be sure to include the source information in your bibliography or works cited page at the end of your report.

Now it's your turn. Below are two different sources and quotations. Put each set together into its own sentence, using any of the formats in this skill or any formats your teacher may give you. Use the spaces below:

Author: Dexter Foxx
Book: *Wild Fowl I Have Known*
Page used: 13
Quotation: "Chicken, duck, goose, pheasant—each has its own delicate taste. I would not turn up my pointed snout at any of these delicious treats."

_____

_____

_____

Author: Dexter Foxx
Web site: www.wildfowl.com
Quotation: "Wild turkeys, though the hardest to run down, are the most succulent creatures for a holiday feast."

_____

_____

_____

Skill 14: **Head** and **Feet** again

Remember the lessons in "Opinions—You've Got Them" on how to write the introduction and the conclusion of your paper? If you don't remember how to write these two important paragraphs, turn to pages 21-25 and read this information again.

You will begin your introduction with something to hook your reader: an interesting **statement, fact, quotation, question,** or **story**. You will most likely end your introduction with your main idea (thesis statement).

Below are two sample introductions for a science paper on how trees are made into paper. Please check the box next to the paragraph that is the better way to begin a paper.

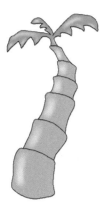

☐ This paper is about how trees are made into paper. I will show you the process from beginning to end. There are many interesting steps.

☐ How can something so rough, huge, and heavy turn into something as smooth, thin, and light as a balloon? Each year, thousands of specially planted trees are harvested to provide paper products for us. Every calendar, diary, poster, paper plate, and photo paper began its life as a tree. Join me as I take you on a tour of the fascinating process.

Which box did you check? I hope you checked the second one. It begins with a question and makes the reader curious about the topic.

Below are two sample conclusions. Please check the box next to the paragraph that is the better way to end a science paper about different kinds of seeds. Then read the next page.

☐ If you looked at a seed and tried to figure out what would grow from it, you might not be able to. Its size and shape show no clues about the plant that will emerge. From a pinecone as small as a pen cap, a huge redwood can grow! There is nothing as delicate, as beautiful, or as full of promise as a seed. Take one home and plant it today.

☐ So, those are the different kinds of seeds and the many ways God made them to be transported and planted. Weeds, flowers, trees, and even grasses all have seeds.

Which box did you check this time? I don't know about you, but this choice is a no-brainer for me. I would rather read the first conclusion.

Now it's your turn. You get to grade a textbook. Open your science or history book to any chapter and read the *first* paragraph. Then answer these questions:

1. Was the paragraph interesting or dull? What made it so?

2. Did it include an interesting statement, fact, quotation, question, or story? If so, what?

3. What would you do to this paragraph to improve it? (No fair saying you would take it out!)

4. Based on your knowledge of how to write an introduction, what grade would you give the writer of the textbook?

Skill 15: **Questions** and **Answers**

Question: What's the difference between an essay and a report?

Answer: An **essay** is a collection of the writer's *thoughts* and *opinions* on a particular subject. The following men are famous for their essays:

➡ Sir Francis Bacon, who lived from 1561-1626, wrote an essay titled "On Travel." It contains advice to young Englishmen traveling to foreign countries. Bacon encourages them to experience all they can in that country but not to bore everyone by constantly talking about it when they return home.

➡ In the 1800s, Henry David Thoreau wrote an essay titled "Walking." In it he wrote that people only walked in order to get from here to there; they weren't walking anymore to enjoy the beauties of nature. He thought this was a shame.

➡ In 1897, Mark Twain published "How to Tell a Story," an essay on—guess what?—how to tell a story. He was very good at telling stories and wanted to teach other people how to do it well too.

You may have written essays in the past. Have you ever written on the beauties of a forest, what the most important thing in the world is to you, or why learning another language is a good thing? Your essays included your thoughts and opinions on a subject.

A **report**, on the other hand, is a collection of *facts* about a certain topic. To write a report, you learn about your topic by doing some research and by taking notes. A report can be on Switzerland, Paul Revere's life, the oceans, dolphins, the solar system, democracy, or a book you have read for school.

Question: What is the difference between fiction and nonfiction?

Answer: **Fiction** is made-up stories. *Peter Pan* is fiction. *The Hobbit* is fiction. O. Henry's short story "The Ransom of Red Chief" is fiction. Any parables Jesus told are under the category of fiction. Even though they are meant to teach us true things, he made them up. They contain characters, conflict, and a plot. However, a story told in the Bible *about* Jesus and what he did is *nonfiction* because it is true.

Nonfiction is true and has facts in it. It can be a newspaper article on last night's ballgame, the instructions on how to operate your new DVD player, an article in *Clubhouse* on friends, a biography of C.S. Lewis, or a book teaching people how to write. Some of these will contain stories to make their point, but the stories will be true stories—stories that have actually happened to real people. The chapter about David and Goliath in the Bible is a story, but it is *nonfiction* because it is a true story, not a made-up one. Your reports, incidentally, are nonfiction.

Question: Can a paragraph have only one sentence in it?

Answer: Yes, but only once in a great while. In a report, the concluding paragraph will sometimes have one sentence if it makes sense that way. Rarely will a paragraph in the body of your report have just one sentence. If it does, it usually means you didn't do your research.

Question: Is it all right for me to copy the words from a source and put them in my report?

Answer: Only if you put quotation marks around them and tell who said it or what book (or source) you got it from. If you don't give credit to the original source, you are committing plagiarism. Aside from being unfair, it is also illegal. Learn to paraphrase or cite your sources correctly.

Now it's your turn. In the space below, write what was new or interesting to you in these questions and answers. Be specific.

Skill 16: The **Assignment**

CHOOSE ONE:
(Use as many sources as you want but only **one** Internet source.)

☐ Choose an animal you love. Do the research. Write a report of at least 300 words on it. Include a bibliography.

☐ Choose an animal you can't stand. Do the research. Write a report of at least 300 words on it. Include a bibliography.

☐ Choose a country you would like someday to visit. Do the research. Write a report of at least 300 words on it. Include a bibliography.

☐ Choose a subject of interest to you. Do the research. Write a report of at least 300 words on it. Include a bibliography.

A suggested writing schedule:

Day 1   ☐ Decide on your topic and narrow it down. Go to the library for books.

Days 2 - 5   ☐ Read your books, make your bibliography, and take notes. Adjust your narrowed-down topic if you have to. Write your main idea (thesis statement).

Day 6   ☐ Organize your thoughts and notes. Use an outline, a list, a cluster, or a Greek temple.

Days 7-9   ☐ Write your report.

Day 10   ☐ Proofread three separate times for mistakes. Make a neat copy.

Remember to use the **Mistake Medic** on page 238 in **YOUR LOCKER!**

A Biography

Skill 1: It's all about—Who?

You've probably read a few biographies for school or for your own enjoyment. Maybe you have read some autobiographies too. What's the difference between a biography and an autobiography?

- A **biography** is a true story of a person's life. It is not written by that person but by someone else. For example, many people have written biographies of Mark Twain's interesting life.

- An **autobiography** is a true story of a person's life written by that person. For example, Mark Twain wrote his own amusing autobiography about his life.

Now it's your turn. Think back and remember some of the biographies or autobiographies you have read in the past few years. Write the names of the people the books were about in the spaces below. Put a check mark next to the books you liked. Cross off the ones you didn't like. Then turn the page.

1.

2.

3.

4.

Now it's your turn again. Below are the names of ten famous people. The following sentences could be the first lines in their biographies. Match the number of the sentence with the correct person.

_____Sir James Barrie (*Peter Pan*)   _____Michelangelo

_____Beverly Cleary (*Ramona* books)   _____Walt Disney

_____Theodor Geisel (Dr. Seuss)   _____Helen Keller

_____Abraham Lincoln   _____Martin Luther

_____J.C. Penney   _____George Washington

1. He firmly believed that nothing important happened to a boy after the age of twelve.

2. He never wanted to be the president of America. In fact, like his older brother, he wanted to join the British navy.

3. She was born perfectly healthy.

4. After his butcher shop failed, he wondered if he would ever be a successful businessman.

5. When she lived in Portland, Oregon, as a young girl with her mother, she lived near Klickitat Street.

6. Twenty-seven companies rejected his first book before he found a publisher. Later, a friend gave him a list of words and a challenge: "Write a book with this list of simple words so that children can learn to read by it." He was stumped; he didn't know what to do—until he noticed that some of the words rhymed.

7. Despite his church's rules, he married a nun and translated the Bible from Latin into his own language—German.

8. He once said that he was never so content as when he had a chisel in his hand.

9. At seven years old, he loved to draw, often sketching pictures of animals or nature instead of finishing his homework. He even sold his pictures to friends and neighbors. Thus began a career that would last the rest of his life.

10. Though he did not know it, he had a disease that could have killed him.

We think of lives as **chronological**. In other words, we think of them in a "time" order: born, lived, did some stuff, and died. But biographies don't have to be written in that order.   Look at the game you just finished and answer these questions:

1. How many of these biographies begin with the person's birth?

2. Why is her birth mentioned?

3. Some of these biographies begin with a hint about how the person became famous. Why is that a good way to start a biography?

Skill 2: Let me count the **Ways**, part I

You can do a lot of fun things with biographies. After all, you are writing to teach, explain, inspire, and even entertain.

Below is a list of eight different ways to write a biography. When you finish reading the list, read the examples on the next two pages.

Different Ways to Write Biographies

1. Write about a person's accomplishments: If he hadn't been born, then we wouldn't have _____ (or we wouldn't know _____).

2. Write about the part of his childhood that is the key to his future accomplishments.

3. Write about the life of someone you respect. Use her accomplishments and difficulties to show why you respect her.

4. Write about the life of someone you don't respect. Don't choose a family member or neighbor! Choose a person from history or a person in the public eye today. Write about his negative accomplishments or his character flaws to show why you don't respect him.

5. Write a "Who Am I?" in which you tell interesting things about the person but save the name for near the end of your biography.

6. Write about an important or pivotal day in the life of your person. Show what happened and how it changed him.

7. Write about a person's spiritual development throughout his life.

8. Write an imaginary page from your person's journal, diary, or letter. Show the reader what your person was like. Include facts.

EXAMPLES

1. **Write about a person's accomplishments.** If Alexander Graham Bell hadn't been born, we wouldn't have telephones. (You would write about his life and his work to invent the telephone.)

If Mary Anderson hadn't applied for her patent in 1905, we wouldn't have windshield wipers. (You would write about her life and the things about it that made her invent this practical device.)

If Sir Isaac Newton hadn't been born, we wouldn't know about the law of gravity. (You would write about his life and how he discovered the law of gravity as it applies to Earth and the planets.)

If Ruth Handler hadn't invented this particular toy in 1959, the world would be without Barbie dolls. (You would write about her life and her interest in developing a new kind of doll.)

Now it's your turn. Think of someone who would fit this category of biography. Write what we wouldn't have or wouldn't know if he or she hadn't been born. Person: _____

Information: _____

2. **Write about the part of his childhood that is the key to his future accomplishments.** The part of St. Patrick's childhood that was the key to his future is how people who lived in what is now Ireland kidnapped him. Years after he escaped, he returned to the people and the island to tell them about the one true God. (You would write his adventures and tell the reader how that affected him and how he made his decision to return.)

Now it's your turn. Think of someone whose life was changed or directed by something that happened in his or her youth. Write who it is and what the event was. Person: _____

Event: _____

3. **Write about someone you respect.** The biography on the next page was written by a girl in the eighth grade. It contains 369 words. This is someone she respects.

The Dauntless Woman

Florence Nightingale's early years were full of study, balls, and social activity. She was born in Florence, Italy, and was named for the town. Her mother was a lady of finery, enjoying and entertaining society. Still, Florence was a studious girl, and the occupation she enjoyed most was helping those in need or those who were ill. This agitated her mother. Her father, a strict tutor, expected much from his two daughters— teaching them many languages in addition to mathematics, history, and philosophy.

When Florence was older, she traveled to many countries all over Europe. She was even presented to the queen of England.

In 1854, the Crimean War broke out. It involved Britain, Russia, and France. During this war, the British secretary of war asked Florence to assist with the hospital in Scutari, Turkey. She agreed and promptly set out for the hospital with thirty-eight nurses accompanying her. Here, Florence encountered difficulty. The doctors were totally opposed to her cleaning up the hospital. The hospital was very filthy and infested with rats and mice, making it very inhospitable to homesick soldiers. Despite the doctors' opposition, she pushed on, and after much labor, along with her nurses, Florence accomplished much. Adding to her vital toil, Miss Nightingale spent hours going about with a lamp, aiding and encouraging the wounded troops. Thus she was, and is, remembered as the "Lady of the Lamp" for her service during the Crimean War.

During Florence's later years, she wrote many letters in addition to a few books. In Florence's school for nurses, the nurses were called Nightingales. Nightingales were trained and sent to various countries to serve there. Upon hearing of a certain Nightingale's destination, Florence would send some flowers ahead to delight the nurse upon her arrival. In 1861, an illness that hung about till her death came upon her, leaving her mostly at home—an invalid. When she was quite elderly, she received a medal from the queen for her honorable deeds. Florence Nightingale died in 1910, a woman who gave all for her God and her country. She was a woman of integrity, endurance, and someone who loved helping people. For these, I admire her.

Now it's your turn. Think of someone you admire. Write the name and two reasons why you admire this person.

Name: _____

1.

2.

Skill 3: Let me count the **Ways**, part II

4. Write about someone that you don't respect. Below is a biography about someone the writer doesn't respect. It contains 373 words.

I Don't Like Him

I like to read his books; I like his humor. But if I ever met him, I know I wouldn't like him. Who am I talking about? Samuel Clemens, better known as Mark Twain.

Sam was a spoiled boy who always got his way. He wrote in his autobiography that he and one or two of his friends were the models for Tom Sawyer. Tom always found a way to do what he wanted, even if it meant lying, cheating, or hurting someone. He treated his Aunt Polly with disrespect and didn't repent.

Sam was also very lazy. When he worked in a silver mine, he could only bring himself to work two weeks while all the rest of the men worked every day for months. He wrote in his autobiography that he just couldn't stand the physical labor of mining, so he sat around at the camp.

When I read his books, I can tell that he questioned God. In *The Mysterious Stranger*, a book he wrote late in life, he was very angry with God. He was cynical and refused to believe that God loved him and cared about him. Mr. Clemens blamed God for all the bad things that happened in his life. And he really did have some bad things happen to him too.

His younger brother died from burns he got in a steamboat boiler explosion. Two of his dear daughters died of illnesses. He went bankrupt when a business venture failed. Later, his wife died of an illness, also. He was devastated, and he blamed God.

I don't dislike him because he blamed God. I dislike him because he was an angry man who had a lot of pride. And it was his pride that kept him from God.

Many people who bought Samuel Clemens' books when he first wrote them believed that he didn't really care about what they cared about. They thought that he just wanted to make fun of the things that were important to them. We have lost that idea today because he is funny, and we like funny things.

But I would not like him if I met him. He would be a bitter, self-centered, angry, cynical man. And that isn't funny.

Now it's your turn. Is there someone you have read about or heard about that you don't respect? Write the name and give two reasons why you don't respect that person. Then turn the page.

NAME: _____

1.

2.

5. **Write a "Who Am I?"** This biography was written by a boy in the sixth grade. It contains 347 words. See if you can guess who the man is before you get to the end.

A Great Sculptor

He was born in 1475 in the small town of Caprese, Italy. Today, Caprese is called Tuscany.

One day his mother got very ill and couldn't nurse him anymore. Because of this, he had to be given away to someone who had children and could nurse him.

The woman's husband was a stonecutter. Each day the boy would help the stonecutter collect marble from the quarries nearby.

Finally, when he was ten years old, he returned to his home. Unfortunately, his mother had died.

He learned a lot from the stonecutter and enjoyed working with stone and marble. His father, however, wanted him to be a wealthy businessman. The boy was not interested and often neglected his studies so that he could spend time drawing. At age thirteen, his dad finally let him take painting lessons from Domenic Ghirlandaio in the village of Florence. He loved studying the human form. He was also able to perfectly sketch anything he had seen only once. Domenic once said, "This boy knows more than I do."

A man named Lorenzo de Medici invited the boy to live at his palace in Florence where he could study with some of the finest sculptors and artists of the day. At age seventeen, he completed his first masterpiece, the *Madonna of the Stairs.*

His works looked like they could move, and they seemed peaceful. In 1534, he started his most famous painting, *The Last Judgment.* Seven years later he completed the paintings that are on the ceiling of the Sistine Chapel in Rome.

He was very old in 1564 and not expected to live much longer. He died while he was working on a pietà for himself. Unfortunately, he wasn't a Christian. On his deathbed, he told a friend, "I regret that I have not done enough for the salvation of my soul." Can you guess who this great person was? If you guessed Michelangelo di Buonaroti Simoni, you're right. He has left the world some of the most beautiful pieces of art and might have been the greatest sculptor of all time.

Now it's your turn. Write the name of someone interesting you could use for a "Who am I?" biography.

NAME: _____

6. Write about an important or pivotal day in the life of your person. Go back to the exciting day in First Lady Dolley Madison's life when she grabbed a famous painting of George Washington from the White House and saved it from the invading British army in the War of 1812. Or put yourself in a time machine and travel to an important day in Julius Caesar's life.

Now it's your turn. Think of an important day in someone's life. Who is the

person? _____

And what is the day? _____

_____

7. Write about someone's spiritual development. It is interesting to write about someone's spiritual development if that person changed a lot during his lifetime. It would be fascinating to learn about C.S. Lewis and write about how he used to look down on Christians but later became one.

Now it's your turn. Think of someone who had a life-changing, spiritual turn-

around. _____

8. Write an imaginary page from your person's journal, diary, or letter. What would it be like to write a journal entry for a famous scientist on the day he discovered something important? Get all the facts and load the journal with those facts as though he were writing it himself.

Now it's your turn. What important person and day would you write a journal

entry for? Person: _____

Day: _____

Anyone will look pretty good in his own autobiography. But a magazine article or another book might tell a different story. The more sources you use, the more accurate your biography will be. For example:

> It is important to get information from as many sources as you can.

Before the Japanese bombed Pearl Harbor in World War II, many Americans didn't want the U.S. to get involved in the war. Charles Lindbergh, the famous aviator, was one of those people. He believed that the war was a European one and should stay that way. You can read what he thought about the war in his autobiography and in his wife's interesting books (Anne Morrow Lindbergh).

However, if you read the magazine and newspaper articles of the day, you will find that some people thought Charles Lindbergh was a Nazi and that he wanted the Germans to win the war. They thought that his trips to Germany—and the medal the Germans gave him—were the reasons he didn't want the U.S. to get involved.

And for some reason, Charles failed to mention in his autobiography that some of his trips to Germany after the war were to visit the mother of his three illegitimate children. Hmmm…

Remember to get all the angles—read many sources.

Skill 4: Ho-Hum

Nobody wants to read a biography that is boring. In fact, if all biographies were boring, no one would write or read them.

What makes a biography interesting?

- The person is famous.
- The person did something interesting.
- The person overcame tremendous difficulties.

If you walk through a grocery checkout aisle, you will see just how interested we are in famous singers, actors, musicians, sports figures, politicians, and other celebrities who have their pictures on magazines.

If someone did something interesting (founded Microsoft, invented a Frisbee™, or walked on the moon), we want to hear about his life and how he accomplished this great task.

If someone overcame tremendous difficulties (became a president even though he had polio, wrote a book when she thought she was dying of tuberculosis, or showered friends and neighbors with her poems even though she was a recluse), we want to read about her and how she overcame her problems.

All of these examples are taken from the lives of real people. Bill Gates founded Microsoft, Walter Morrison invented the Frisbee™ from pie tins of the Frisbie Baking Company, and many men have walked on the moon.

Franklin Delano Roosevelt was the president who had polio and finished his time in office in a wheelchair, Jessamyn West wrote *The Friendly Persuasion* while on her back with tuberculosis, and Emily Dickinson was the poetic hermit.

It is your job to make your person sound interesting.

Explain what your person has accomplished. Tell the story of how hard the problem was and how your person overcame it. Hook your reader and keep him reading. Avoid a boring recital of facts.

Now it's your turn. Brainstorm a short list of famous people who interest you, who have done something interesting, or who have overcome tremendous difficulties. Write your ideas as they come to you in the space below.

Skill 5: The **Assignment**

CHOOSE **ONE**:

☐ Write a simple chronological biography of a famous person, living or dead. Word count: at least 300 words.

☐ Write a biography using one of the eight ways mentioned in this chapter. Word count: at least 300 words.

☐ Create a different way to write a biography and check it with your teacher. Then write the biography. Word count: at least 300 words.

☐ Write your autobiography. Word count: at least 300 words.

A suggested writing schedule:

Day 1   ⇨ Decide on the person. Go to the library for books. (Or check the books and then decide.)

Days 2 - 5   ⇨ Read your books and take notes. Decide on the type of biography you want to write.

Day 6   ⇨ Organize your thoughts and notes. Use an outline, list, cluster, or Greek temple.

Days 7-9   ⇨ Write the biography.

Day 10   ⇨ Proofread three separate times for mistakes. Make a neat copy.

Remember to use the **Mistake Medic** on page 238 in **YOUR LOCKER**!

A Book Report

Skill 1: I read it—Really!

A book report? I can hear the groans.

This chapter, however, is going to make it simple and maybe—just maybe—a tiny bit enjoyable.

Most book reports are written on **books of fiction**: *Treasure Island, Journey to the Center of the Earth, The Jungle Book*, etc. You can write a book report on a nonfiction book, too, but you are not going to for this course.

The skills you use to write a book report will be a bonus to you; they will help you evaluate what you read. You will become a detective, a private eye.

There are two things that go into a book report:

- The **book**

- Your **opinion** of it

Before we go any further, we have to review something you are probably familiar with. Every book is made up of ingredients. Those ingredients are called **elements**. Every short story, parable, fairy tale, play, and novel has these *elements*. If it didn't, the story wouldn't be a story.

Can you guess what some of those elements are?

Get your favorite **fiction** book, or a fiction book you are familiar with. If it is not with you, simply think of a book you have read. You will need it in this skill and the next two. Turn the page to review story elements.

Story Elements

➡   Setting
➡   Characters
➡   Plot
➡   Conflict
➡   Theme

These are the five main ingredients—or elements—that go into any good story. There are other elements, but we are not going to discuss them in this section. Below is a description of **setting**, **characters**, and **plot**. Skill 2 deals with conflict and theme. You probably know most of this, but stay with it anyway.

➡ **SETTING:** The time and the place of the story are called the setting.

> *Island of the Blue Dolphins* by Scott O'Dell happens in the early 1800s on an island off the coast of California.

> *The Lion, the Witch, and the Wardrobe* by C. S. Lewis happens in England during World War II and in Narnia during a perpetual winter.

Now it's your turn. Refer to your favorite or familiar fiction book. What is its setting? _____

➡ **CHARACTERS:** The characters are the people (or animals) in the story. Each character will be a certain age, gender, and intelligence. He or she will also have a definite personality and be driven by a goal.

The main characters can be divided into two categories: **protagonist** and **antagonist**. The *protagonist* is normally the person or animal you are rooting for.

> The main character in *Bambi* is the protagonist because you want Bambi to live and be successful. The main character in *A Little Princess* by Frances Hodgson Burnett is Sara Crewe. Sara is a protagonist because you want her to escape Miss Minchin's meanness; you want her to find happiness.

Sometimes the protagonist isn't a good guy. It is rare, but occasionally writers make a bad guy the protagonist. You will see this when you read *Macbeth* by Shakespeare. Macbeth is a main character and desires something wicked right from the beginning. However, you keep hoping he'll do the right thing.

The **antagonist** is the person or thing making most of the trouble. Each story will have more than one *antagonist*. The protagonist will want something (love, safety, money, help for his family, success in a sport, friends, etc.). The antagonist will try to keep him from getting it.

Bambi has two main antagonists: "He" (humans) and forces of nature such as fire and winter. **Sara Crewe** battles loneliness, grief at losing her father, some nasty students, cold, hunger, and Miss Minchin's harshness. Notice that only two of these are characters—the students and Miss Minchin—but all of them are her antagonists.

In *The Lion, the Witch, and the Wardrobe*, **Lucy**, a protagonist, wants someone to believe that she isn't lying. **Edmond**, another protagonist, wants Turkish Delights and is selfish. Even though he does mean things, we want him to turn out all right. The **White Witch**, an antagonist, wants to reign in Narnia forever. She is very mean, can't be trusted, and makes all kinds of trouble for the four Pevensie children. The **perpetual winter** is also an antagonist—a force that hinders the protagonists in many ways.

Now it's your turn. Who are your book's characters? Write down three or four main ones and say a little about each. Label the protagonist(s) and antagonist(s).

1.   3.

2.   4.

Now turn the page.

➡️ **PLOT:** The plot is the action or events in the story. It's what the characters do and what happens to them.

The plot of *The Lion, the Witch, and the Wardrobe* can be summed up in 37 words: "Four English children find a land where animals talk and it is always winter but never Christmas. They get separated and have to fight a witch before the lion Aslan returns and saves them and the land."

The plot of *The Hobbit* can be summed up in 23 words: "A hobbit, an imaginary creature who hates adventures, is chosen by a wizard to help dwarfs find their treasure that a dragon stole."

Now it's your turn. Sum up the plot of your book in 40 words or less. Tell what the main character *does* during the story and what the major events are.

_____

_____

_____

_____

In Skill 2 you will review **conflict** and **theme** from the element list. Use the same fiction book in Skill 2 that you used to answer the above questions.

Skill 2: Story **Elements**, continued

➡ **CONFLICT:** Characters will have conflicts (troubles, problems, struggles), including internal problems as well as problems outside themselves. These difficulties are the antagonists—the people, obstacles, or forces that characters have to overcome. In any good story, the characters will have to battle more than one problem. The characters want something, but the antagonists are keeping them from getting it. This creates a tension or a conflict. Conflicts can be summed up in these five ways:

- <u>The character against himself.</u> Strangely enough, a character can be his own worst enemy. Maybe he lies, is jealous, won't walk away when he's called a chicken, doubts his own abilities, is marked with a scar, or lets a past failure conquer him. These are internal difficulties he's fighting against (or giving in to).

  In *The Hobbit*, some of Bilbo Baggins' internal problems are that he hates adventures and loves the comfort of his home and routine.

- <u>The character against a person.</u> There is at least one person who gives the protagonist trouble. It might be an unkind friend, a bully, or, in many modern books, a parent.

    In *The Hobbit*, Bilbo and the main dwarf are always fighting. Later, Bilbo has to deal with Gollum and the dragon Smaug, both nasty characters who would like to see him dead.

- <u>The character against society.</u> Sometimes the protagonist has to battle a whole group of people and perhaps even a set of rules. Think of African Americans in the South during the time of slavery. It was illegal to teach them to read or write, and anyone who found a runaway slave had to return him or her to the owner. Those rules and the groups of people who held them are called "society."

    The slaves in *Uncle Tom's Cabin* struggle against a whole society and the way it thinks. A Jew in Hitler's Nazi Germany ran into many of the same problems. It wasn't just one person who created problems but a whole group of people and the way they thought. You can see this clearly in *Anne Frank: The Diary of a Young Girl*.

    In *The Hobbit,* Bilbo has problems with relatives and other hobbits in his shire who look down on him because they think hobbits shouldn't have adventures. Their way of thinking holds him back.

- <u>The character against nature.</u> The protagonist will have to overcome some physical difficulty. Does he have to live on his own for a year, cross a river full of vicious piranhas, survive an earthquake, or climb a mountain range to get his family to safety? These are all physical or nature problems.

  In *The Hobbit,* Bilbo fights fatigue and cold, mountains, giant spiders, dark and nasty woods, and many more physical difficulties.

- <u>The character against God.</u> At times, the character is fighting with God or with something God told him to do. This conflict doesn't appear in all stories, as the other ones do.

  Jonah, in the Bible, constantly is fighting with God. In *Silas Marner* by George Eliot, Silas doubts the goodness of God when terrible things happen to him. In *Robinson Crusoe* by Daniel Defoe, Crusoe first blames God for the shipwreck but later comes to love God.

Now it's your turn.   What are your main character's two biggest problems? List them. Then label them as "Character against _____."

1.

2.

THEME: Themes are lessons, thoughts, or ideas about life that authors write into their stories. They could be as simple as "Friendship helps overcome great difficulties" or "Forgiveness works better than revenge." Most authors want to tell their readers something they've learned about life. That's why they're writing. The interesting thing is that you can read a book and see one theme, and your friend can read the same book and see another theme. With some themes, the author writes them into the story. Others you will see because of your own experiences and insights.

  In *The Lion, the Witch, and the Wardrobe,* one possible theme is that your selfishness not only gets *you* into trouble but it also puts *others* in danger as well.

In *The Hobbit,* one theme is that doing new and brave exploits, especially if you have the help of your friends, is a good thing.

Now it's your turn again.   What is one theme in your book? In other words, what is the author trying to say through the story, or what is something helpful that you learned from your book? Answer in the space below.

If you were to write a book, what main idea would you like your reader to understand? Use the space below to answer.

Skill 3: The **Book** and my **Opinion** of it

You learned in Skill 1 that there are two things that go into a book report: the *book* and your *opinion* of it. There are a few more things to say about the book before we discuss your opinion of it.

Are there any **special features** in the book? For instance, are the *descriptions* very good? Is the *dialogue* witty? Does it have a great *plot* with lots of interesting twists to it? Does the author use good *similes* ("He was **as crazy as** a fox with his tail on fire.")? Is there *humor*? Are there any *symbols* in the book?

Symbols? What are those?

A *symbol* is any ordinary object that makes sense by itself but means something more in the story. Read the chart below for examples of symbols:

SYMBOL	WHAT IT COULD REPRESENT
A country's flag	bravery, patriotism, loyalty, honor
A candle	love, friendship, remembrance, warmth
A ring	love, eternity
A swamp	danger, temptation
A ship	adventure, travel, a whole country
A pillar of fire by night	God's presence among the Israelites
Manna	God's ability to provide for our needs
A raven	death, sorrow, gloomy times
An eagle	freedom, strength, adventure

Here's an example of a symbol in a book:

In *The King's Fifth* by Scott O'Dell, the Indian girl Zia wears a hat that is bordered with red pompoms and little silver bells. The silver bells make a nice sound as she walks. When she walks into Estéban's life, her presence and the little bells cheer and comfort him. When Estéban is led away by his greed, Zia walks away, and he hears the sound of the jingling bells moving into the distance. It is a sad time in the book. What do the bells mean? What do they symbolize? They may symbolize friendship. They may be symbols of Estéban's goodness. When he is good, he has the bells; when he is bad, the bells leave. Their absence tips us off that he has gone over the edge.

Colors can also be used as symbols. What might they mean? If someone is wearing green, she could be peaceful or envious. If red keeps showing up at important times in the book, the author might be using it as a clue that something noteworthy is about to happen.

Now it's your turn.   Think of two everyday things that can be used as symbols. Write them and what they could be used to represent.

1.

2.

Now it's your turn again. Using the book you referred to in Skills 1 and 2, think of a symbol the author might have used. Not every book has one, but many books you read for school do. What is the symbol and what might it mean?

Symbol: _____

What it could mean: _____

_____

Now we can finally talk about **your opinion** of the book. When you mention your opinion in your book report, you will not say, "I liked it," or "I couldn't stand it." You will need to be specific and mention what you liked or didn't like. Were the *characters* shallow and predictable? Was the *plot* dull, with little action? Was the *conflict* so intense that you worried about the character? Did you like the *humor*? Come up with good reasons for your opinion.

Now it's your turn again.   What did you think of your book? Like it? Couldn't stand it? Liked some of it but not the rest? Write your opinion and reason.

OPINION: _____

WHY:

Skill 4: Making it Easy

Use the form in this skill to organize your thoughts as you read any book and prepare for the report. You may copy these pages as often as you need to for any book reports you do in school.

In the Book Report Form, *type of book* means the **genre**, pronounced zhahn'-ruh. *Genre* is a fancy name for what kind of book you are reading: mystery, adventure, historical fiction, comedy, science fiction, fantasy, biography, folk and fairy tale, western, young adult, etc. All of these are examples of different genres.

Try to figure out what type of book you are reading, but if you can't, don't sweat it.

The form below is labeled according to paragraphs you will write in your book report. In Skill 5, you will read a report written by a boy in the seventh grade who used the following form to organize his thoughts. One girl student said that using this form to write a book report is so easy that it almost feels like cheating. Read the form here and on the next four pages and see if you agree.

Book Report Form

PARAGRAPH 1:

Title of book: _____

Type of book (genre): _____

Year it was first published: _____

Author: _____

(form continues on next page)

PARAGRAPHS 1 AND 2:

Setting. Identify the time and place: _____

_____

Main characters. Label the protagonists and antagonists and give a short description of each. Include page numbers:

1.

2.

3.

Conflicts. List the main character's biggest problems:

1.

2.

3.

(form continues on next page)

PARAGRAPH 2:

Plot. The story begins when

The story gets bad when

The story is the very worst—and the main character has to make a major decision—when

The story ends when

Sum up the plot (action—what the character *does*) in 40 words or less:

(form continues on next page)

PARAGRAPH 3:

Theme. What does the author say through this book? Use examples and page numbers:

Short author biography. (Any biographical information that relates to the theme will go in this paragraph.)

PARAGRAPH 4:

Special features. Note great descriptions, plot twists, similes, symbols, etc. Use examples and page numbers:

(form continues on next page)

PARAGRAPH 5:

My opinions

Something that makes the book strong:

Something that makes the book weak:

The character I most strongly identified with is _____

because _____

_____

_____

What I learned from this book:

I ☐ liked   ☐ didn't like   this book because _____

_____

_____

_____

Other comments:

Skill 5: The actual Report

Here is a simple and interesting way to write a book report using the Book Report Form:

- Paragraph 1
    Begin with an interesting first sentence that will draw the reader into your report. Then describe the main character and her life in the beginning of the story before everything falls apart. Remember to include the setting, title, author, and genre.

- Paragraph 2
    Tell what happens to the main character that changes everything for her. Describe a few of the characters in her life, especially the ones who are helpful and the ones who are troublesome. Describe the main character's life as she faces her new problem. Tell enough of the plot to get your reader interested in the book, but don't tell how it ends!

- Paragraph 3
    Talk about the theme of the book—what the author says through the story. Use examples of where the author put the message. Use short quotations from the book to show the reader how the author wove the theme into the story. Include biographical information that shows how the writer learned the theme in his own life, if necessary.

- Paragraph 4
    Show the special features here. Write about them or describe them to the reader. Use short examples from the book.

- Paragraph 5
    Explain your opinion and why you hold it. Use examples or short quotations from the book. Your last sentence should sum up the book and its ideas or sum up your opinion of the book in an interesting way.

Read the book report by a seventh-grade boy on the next page. It contains 361 words. He used the Book Report Form in Skill 4 when he took his notes, but he listed the publishing information separately, at the top left of his paper. Your teacher will tell you which way to do it.

Check what this fellow did. Did he follow the suggested paragraphs on this page?

> You may use *short* examples or *short* quotations from the book. Longer ones are a form of cheating because you are relying on the author of your book to fill out your word count for you.

Book Report
By _____
Due May 15, 20__
Abandoned on the Wild Frontier
Authors: Dave and Neta Jackson
Historical Fiction

    In a matter of one day, Gil's life changed forever. When Gilbert Hamilton was three years old, his mother was kidnapped, and his father was killed by Saukenuk Indians in the War of 1812. So he was forced to live with his Aunt Edith, his Uncle George, and his cousin Robert. After living with them for ten years, he met a circuit preacher named Peter Cartwright.

    When Gil was thirteen, he began to wonder whether his mother was dead or alive. He became determined to find her. He begged his aunt and uncle to allow him to move to Illinois with the Cartwright family to look for his mother. Gil's compassionate aunt thought he should go, but his stubborn uncle wouldn't let him. In the end, he got to go anyway. After living in Illinois for about six months, he finally went north to search for his mother. But sadly, he returned to Illinois without finding her. Will Gil ever see his long lost mother again?

    The authors of this book, Dave and Neta Jackson, successfully taught the reader that persistence pays off in the end. In the process of telling a fictional story about Gilbert Hamilton, the authors also tell the true story of circuit preacher Peter Cartwright, who traveled from place to place preaching the gospel.

    It's really neat how the authors included characters that you can relate to: a stubborn uncle, a compassionate aunt, a boy who felt like he was unimportant, and a boy with a crush. It's also cool how, after all of Gil's hardships, he came to know the Lord because he realized that he couldn't do everything himself.

    Reading how a young boy could be abandoned on the wild frontier and still have the strength to press on is very encouraging. You won't be able to put this book down because the story will thrill you. It is easy to read. The only bad part about this book is that when you finish it, you will be upset that it is over already, and you'll want to read it again. *Abandoned on the Wild Frontier* will encourage you to keep persisting in your goals.

    If this student had included the title, author, and genre in the text of his report, he would have written something like this for the last sentence in his first paragraph: "All of this happens in the historical fiction *Abandoned on the Wild Frontier* by Dave and Neta Jackson."

Now it's your turn. Answer the questions below.

1. Did this student follow the suggested paragraphs?

2. Do you want to read *Abandoned on the Wild Frontier*?

Skill 6: The **Assignment**

CHOOSE **ONE**:

☐ Write a book report on a favorite book. Use the Book Report Form to organize your notes. Word count: at least 300 words.

☐ Write a book report on a book you don't like. Use the Book Report Form to organize your notes. Word count: at least 300 words.

☐ Write a book report on a book your teacher assigns you. Use the Book Report Form to organize your notes. Word count: at least 300 words.

Book Report Planner

Write the assignment down as your teacher gave it to you:

What you have to do	**Date**
Get two books from the library.	_____
Finish the books and decide which to use.	_____
Fill out the Book Report Form.	_____
Finish your first draft.	_____
Reread and revise.	_____
Get it into its finished form.	_____
THIS IS DUE BY (Fill out this line first and work backward from it.)	_____

Remember to use the **Mistake Medic** on page 238 in **YOUR LOCKER**!

A Book Response

Skill 1: What's **This?**

Many times, a book report is the right thing to do. But what if you are yearning for something different, something more?

There is hope. Try your hand at a **book response** instead of a report. With a *book response*, you can use talents other than writing or use your writing abilities in interesting ways.

Below and on the next page are 15 different things you can do after you have read a book. How many more can you think of?

In Skill 2, you will find examples of some of the responses done by students.

ARTISTIC SKILLS

1. **Draw, paint, or sculpt** an interesting character or scene from the book. Label the picture or include a caption.

2. **Create a mural** with friends. Illustrate a setting or a scene.

3. Make a **3-D scene** in a box (a diorama) to illustrate a section of the story. Use the author's description of that scene. Try to capture the mood too.

4. **Draw a map** for the inside cover of the book, labeling the lands that people in the story traveled in. If it is a journey, show the beginning and the destination. Don't forget the dangerous places. Color your map if you want to.

5. Research the kinds of clothes (or weapons, houses, cars, furniture, etc.) the people in your story might have used. **Draw or paint** pictures of them, **build** a model or replica, or **sew** the clothes.

6. **Act out** an important scene from the book with a friend or two in front of an audience. Use costumes and props.

<u>WRITING SKILLS</u>

7. Make a **report card** for the author. Grade him on the basics: setting, characters, plot, etc. Also grade him on how he began and ended the book, if the book held your attention, if he used similes and metaphors, etc. Include why you gave him those grades and what he can do to improve.

8. Write a **story or poem** of your own based on something you read in the book.

9. Write a **letter to the author**. Ask her something about the book or tell her something. If the author is still living, you can send your letter to the publisher listed on the inside of your book.

10. Write a letter to an **imaginary librarian** telling her why she should buy this book for the library. Tell her a little bit about the book, why it will appeal to other readers, and why you liked it.

11. Write a **blurb** (the part of the story you find on the back cover of the book). Tell enough of the story to get the reader interested—but don't tell the ending!

12. Write a **negative blurb** as on the backs of A Series of Unfortunate Events books, telling the reader why he should *not* read the book. This is using reverse psychology. The more you tell the reader not to read it, the more he will want to.

13. Write a pretend **telephone conversation** between you and a friend. Tell her why you think she would like the story and what you liked about it. Or tell her *not* to read it and what you *didn't* like about it.

14. Read about any **animals** in the book and write a short report or give a short speech on them.

15. Write a **television commercial** for the book. Include what you liked about it. Then read it to an interested audience.

Now it's your turn. Create another book response. _____

_____

Which response from the list above interests you? _____

_____

_____

Skill 2: Some **Examples**

1. **Draw or paint a picture.** A boy in the eighth grade drew this picture after he read *Robinson Crusoe* by Daniel Defoe.

7. **Report card for the author.** A girl in the eighth grade made this report card for *The Witch of Blackbird Pond* by Elizabeth George Speare.

Report Card for Elizabeth George Speare

Title	A+
Plot	A+
Beginning	B-
Ending	A
Blurb	C
Cover design	A
Overall grade	A

Further notes:

The title was very carefully chosen. It was mysterious and very appealing to me as a reader. Great job!

The plot was very good. The suspense was very lightly felt in the beginning and began to build upon itself as the book continued. I didn't want to put the book down.

The beginning was okay. I didn't feel it quite met up to the standards set by the rest of the story. Experiment more!

The ending was really good, but I think it was given away a page too soon.

The blurb did not appeal to me. I do not think it really caught the best of the story.

The cover design fit well with the title. Nice book!

12. **Write a negative blurb.** Below are two examples of a negative blurb. The first one was written by a boy in the seventh grade. His book was *The Call of the Wild* by Jack London. The second one was written by another boy in the seventh grade. His book was *The Magician's Nephew* by C. S. Lewis. Despite the gloomy descriptions, a negative blurb can often be slightly lighthearted, using reverse psychology to interest the reader.

The Call of the Wild

This is a sad story. Would you believe this dog's luck? He is kidnapped from his home in California. Then he is sold and beaten with a club on a train ride. After three days of that train ride, he is sold again, put on a boat, and falls into unconsciousness. When he wakes up, he finds himself in Alaska! And that's just the beginning!

You don't want to read this book. So many bad things happen to this dog. This book is a waste of your time. I do not envy anyone who chooses to read this book, and I leave you with that.

The Magician's Nephew

I'm sorry to say, but if you've decided to read this book, you have made a terrible mistake. This magical book may seem sweet and innocent at first, but it gets scarier and scarier and scarier until it may just give you nightmares.

How would you like to be transported to other worlds by rings, be at the mercy of a witch, be face to face with a lion, or have to live with a madman uncle who thinks he is a magician? Well, that is what Digory and Polly have to endure. So, if you don't want to join Digory and Polly in their troubles, do not open this book!

15. Write a television commercial for the book. A boy in the fifth grade wrote this after reading an Encyclopedia Brown book. It contains 235 words. Do you think he could sell the book?

Encyclopedia Brown Lends a Hand by Donald J. Sobol

I have just read *Encyclopedia Brown Lends a Hand* by Donald J. Sobol. I like Encyclopedia Brown books because I like solving mysteries. I like it because it's lots of different short stories. I especially liked "The Case of the Skunk Ape," where a girl dresses up as a smelly ape and steals a boy's cello case. In "The Case of the Salami Sandwich," a boy loses his sandwich and almost loses his job.

Encyclopedia Brown is the son of the chief of police in Idaville. He helps his dad solve mysteries a lot, and he helps his friends, too. He earns 25 cents for a case. I learned that Encyclopedia Brown has read more books than anyone else in Idaville. He solves all the mysteries in neat ways. His real name is Leroy, but he's stuck with his nickname, Encyclopedia. His main enemy in all the stories is Bugs Meany. Bugs Meany is one of the reasons Encyclopedia has Sally Kimball. Sally is the most athletic girl in Idaville. She is like a bodyguard. She sticks with Encyclopedia wherever he goes.

I would recommend this book to you because it is full of neat mysteries. I have solved a lot of Encyclopedia Brown mysteries, and maybe you can, too. There are lots of Encyclopedia Brown books that I've read. When I grow up, I want to be a detective, too, just like Encyclopedia Brown.

Now it's your turn. There are many different ways to respond to a book for your schoolwork. After seeing the examples, which responses do you like? Write them in the space below.

Skill 3: The **Assignment**

CHOOSE **ONE**:

☐ Decide on an artistic-skill book response and do it.

☐ Decide on a writing-skill book response and do it.

☐ Make up a new response, get it approved by your teacher, and do it.

Book Response Schedule

What you have to do	**Date**
Get two books from the library.	_____
Finish the books and decide which to use.	_____
Decide on a book response.	_____
Finish your first draft (if necessary).	_____
Reread and revise (if necessary).	_____
Put your response into its finished form.	_____
THIS IS DUE BY (Fill out this line first and work backward from it.)	_____

A Newspaper Article

Skill 1: Just the **Facts**, Ma'am

The first thing a good reporter needs to learn is how to report just the facts, not his opinion of the facts. When he includes his opinions with the facts, he is showing his **bias**—his way of thinking and his value judgments.

Here's the difference between a fact and an opinion:

☐ A **fact** can be proven true or false based on the available information.

☐ In an **opinion**, two people can look at the available information and form opposing viewpoints.

What does that mean? Here is an example that will clear things up:

Fact: The music is playing at 70 decibels. (That statement can be proven true or false by measuring the noise level.)
Opinion: The music is too loud/The music isn't loud enough. (Two people can hear the 70 decibels and form opposing viewpoints.)

Read these pairs of sentences on the next page for more examples:

Fact: The elevation of Pikes Peak is 14,110 feet.
Opinion: The Rocky Mountains are beautiful. (That is a value judgment. You may agree with the statement, but the early pioneers who had to cross the rock-strewn mountains in wooden-wheeled wagons through blinding, freezing blizzards might not have thought they were so beautiful.)

Fact: Senator Palmer has served in the Senate for 20 years and has never missed a roll-call vote.
Opinion: We should vote Senator Palmer into office again; he will do a good job. (He is consistent, but what issues does he vote for?)

Fact: James Galway often plays music of different countries.
Opinion: I like to hear James Galway play his lovely flute featuring music from around the world. (I may enjoy flute music, but someone else may find it irritating.)

Fact: Ebenezer Scrooge provided little coal for his office fire, refused to give money to orphans, and thought that all poor people should die "and decrease the surplus population" or go to poorhouses or jails.
Opinion: Ebenezer Scrooge was a mean man, and he was stingy. (He thought he was being reasonable.)

Don't get me wrong. Having opinions is not bad. In fact, you need them in order to navigate the tricky waters of life. In any writing other than newswriting, you are allowed to state your opinions. But putting them in a newspaper article—showing your *bias*—is not supposed to happen.

Do reporters often put their opinions in their articles? Unfortunately, they do. Are they supposed to? No.

Instead of delving into media bias in this lesson, however, you are simply going to identify the difference between a fact and an opinion.

Now it's your turn. Read the sentences below and on the next page. If the sentence is a fact, label it "F." If it is an opinion, label it "O."

_____1. Many famous novel writers began their careers writing for newspapers.

_____2. Writing for a newspaper is a good way to begin a career in novel writing.

_____3. The Beavers won five more games this season than they did last season.

_____4. Mozart's music is better than Bach's.

_____5. *The Cricket in Times Square* is an interesting book.

_____6. The Otters deserve to win the World Series this year. They've worked so hard, and they have the best pitchers in the league.

_____7. I learned a lot from attending the cake-decorating classes.

_____8. You should have your picture taken by Roger Jolly. He takes great pictures.

_____9. The songs our choir is singing this year are the best they've ever been.

_____10. The cost of living is higher in America than it is in Guatemala.

_____11. Our water has a distinctive odor because it has a lot of sulfur in it.

_____12. Covering your mouth when you sneeze is one way to keep from spreading your cold to someone else.

_____13. Thirteen is an unlucky number.

Skill 2: You're the **Reporter**

Many famous novel writers began their careers writing for newspapers. Rudyard Kipling, who wrote *The Jungle Book* and *Kim*, was one of them. Here's a piece of a poem he wrote about something he learned in the newspaper business:

> I keep six honest serving men
> (They taught me all I knew);
> Their names are What and Why and When
> And How and Where and Who.

Kipling wrote the names of his "honest serving men" in that order so they would rhyme. But he would have used them in a newspaper article in a different order—in their order of importance. Below is the inverted triangle reporters often use. The important information is at the top, and the less important is at the bottom:

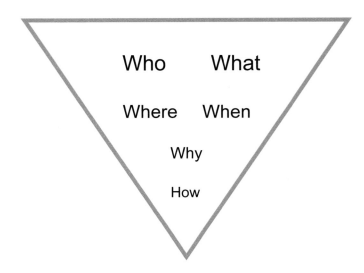

People usually want to read their information in this order:

- ☐ **Who** did it happen to?
- ☐ **What** happened to him?
- ☐ **Where** did it happen?
- ☐ **When** did it happen?
- ☐ **Why** did it happen?
- ☐ **How** did it happen?

Sometimes *how* and *why* switch places with each other, depending on the story.

Here's a silly example of putting all the important information in the right order. It is the first paragraph of an imaginary news article:

> U. S. President Butterfield was hit on the head with a boomerang while visiting the Taronga Zoo in Sydney, Australia, early this morning. Apparently, a caged kangaroo snatched the boomerang from a nearby child and threw it at the president. Zoo officials are now checking with the kangaroo to see if she has been dissatisfied with her surroundings.

It's all in there—who, what, where, when, how, and why. (The *how* came before the *why* in that paragraph.) Here is the same paragraph with the "honest serving men" put in:

> U. S. President Butterfield [who] was hit on the head with a boomerang [what] while visiting the Taronga Zoo in Sydney, Australia [where], early this morning [when]. Apparently, a caged kangaroo snatched the boomerang from a nearby child and threw it at the president [how]. Zoo officials are now checking with the kangaroo to see if she has been dissatisfied with her surroundings [why].

The first sentence or paragraph in a news article is called a **lead**. It answers most of the who, what, when, where, why, and how questions. If it is written well, it will hook the reader and *lead* him into the rest of the article. If the article is short, the lead might be only a sentence long. If the article is a long one, the lead could be as long as a paragraph or two.

Now it's your turn. Think of something interesting that happened in your family, church, community, sports team, choir, camp, etc. Write a lead for an article about the event. Include the five Ws and one H (who, what, where, when, why, and how). Remember to use facts, not opinions.

After you have written your lead, label the five Ws and one H. Use a separate piece of paper.

Skill 3: Under the **Microscope**

Read any well-written newspaper article and you will see a pattern: The lead contains all the important information, the next paragraphs tell the complete story, and the last paragraphs fill in with background information.

The very important information is in the beginning of the article, and the not so important is near the end.

Below is a portion of a news article used with permission from the *Kokomo Tribune* and dated June 22, 2004:

First private spaceflight deemed a success

Manned rocket plane flies 62.2 miles above the earth.

Lead Paragraph

MOJAVE, Calif. (AP) – An ungainly-looking rocket plane punched through the Earth's atmosphere and then glided home to a desert landing Monday in history's first privately financed manned spaceflight – a voyage that could hasten the day when the final frontier is opened up to paying customers.

The rest of the story

Pilot Mike Melvill took SpaceShipOne 62.2 miles above Earth, just a little more than 400 feet above the distance considered to be the boundary of space. The flight lasted just 90 minutes.

The spaceship – with its fat fuselage and spindly white wings – was carried aloft under the belly of a carrier jet. The jet then released the spaceship, and its rocket engine ignited, sending it hurtling toward space at nearly three times the speed of sound. It left a vertical white vapor trail in the brilliant blue sky.

SpaceShipOne touched down in the Mojave Desert at 8:15 a.m. to cheers and applause.

Melvill, 63, said seeing the curvature of the Earth was "almost a religious experience."

"It was really an awesome sight," he said. "It was like nothing I'd ever seen before, and it blew me away."

The flight is an important step toward winning the Ansari X Prize, a $10 million award for the first privately financed three-seat spacecraft to reach an altitude of 62 miles and repeat the feat within two weeks.

Background info

The three-seat requirement demonstrates the capacity for paying customers; the quick turnaround between flights demonstrates reusability and reliability.

Now it's your turn. Below are the first two sentences from the article on the historic space flight. Look for the "six honest serving men." Underline the words that answer who, what, when, where, why, and how; then write who, what, when, where, why, and how over the underlined words. Warning—they may not be in their original order.

MOJAVE, Calif. (AP) – An ungainly-looking rocket plane punched through the Earth's atmosphere and then glided home to a desert landing Monday in history's first privately financed manned spaceflight – a voyage that could hasten the day when the final frontier is opened up to paying customers. Pilot Mike Melvill took SpaceShipOne 62.2 miles above Earth, just a little more than 400 feet above the distance considered to be the boundary of space.

Why isn't the *who* first? Because *who* isn't as important in this particular news event as *what*.

Skill 4: Big **Deal!**

What are these words doing at the end of the first sentence of the news article on page 140 (Skill 3): " – a voyage that could hasten the day when the final frontier is opened up to paying customers"?

That part of the news article is there to show the readers the **significance** of the report (the S). It is the reporter's job to show the reader why that news is important. Otherwise, the readers just might ask, "So what?"

What is the *significance* of the news from Mojave, California? Wasn't that just another rocket that went into outer space? Aren't rockets old news?

The reporter who wrote that article understood that someday, because the rocket was privately funded and not funded by the government (NASA), ordinary people would one day be able to go into outer space. That was the significance of his report.

If you were to write the lead in the *Valley of Elah News* for an important battle that took place there, you might write something like this:

David ben Jesse, with a stunning surprise strategy, defeated the Philistine champion, Goliath of Gath, earlier today in what had been a stalled battle in the Valley of Elah. This is the first time in many years that the Israelites have been able to score a victory against their long-time enemies.

Here is the lead with some of the "serving men" and the S put in:

David ben Jesse [who], with a stunning surprise strategy, defeated the Philistine champion [what], Goliath of Gath, earlier today [when] in what had been a stalled battle in the Valley of Elah [where]. This is the first time in many years that the Israelites have been able to score a victory against their long-time enemies [significance].

The how and why, in this case, would be the rest of the story in the next paragraphs, telling *how* the teenage shepherd and his slingshot brought down a great enemy champion and *why* he did it.

Now it's your turn. Choose another Bible story and read it to get the facts. Then write the lead. Use the "serving men" and include the significance of the event. Label the 5 Ws, the H, and the S. Remember to use facts, not opinions. Use a separate piece of paper.

Skill 5: Fill me In

After you write your lead, you will **finish telling the story** in a chronological order, the order in which the event actually occurred. Because your lead is shortened up to get the essential information in first, the readers will want to know more information about the incident. So you tell the story.

What might the beginning of the rest of the story look like in David ben Jesse's case? Check out the following paragraphs. They follow the lead paragraph about David you read on page 142 (Skill 4).

> Today began as usual for David, who is the shepherd for his father's flocks in Bethlehem. When he reported for duty, however, his father loaded up the donkeys with food and sent David to the battle site, where his three older brothers are soldiers under King Saul's command.
>
> David arrived in time to watch the two armies rush into their battle lines and shout battle cries to each other across the valley. Leaving the grain, bread, and cheeses with the supply commander, David ran to the front lines to find his brothers.
>
> What he found, though, was a Philistine giant who shouted insults at the Israelite army. At the sight of Goliath of Gath, who is over nine feet tall, the Israelite army broke ranks and retreated. David, shocked, found that the giant had been doing this every morning and evening for forty days. This evidently was too much for the shepherd boy. He determined to do something about it.

If you were writing this, you would continue the story, telling about the visit to King Saul and the fight with Goliath. Reread paragraphs two through six from the space-flight story on page 140 (Skill 3). There you find the information about the actual flight and about the pilot, Mike Melvill, along with some quotations from him. That's the rest of the story, the part that didn't fit into the snappy lead.

What is the **background information** you saw in the right column of the space-flight article on page 140 (Skill 3)? The *background information* was about the Ansari X Prize and how to win it. However, you will not be practicing that skill in this workbook.

Now it's your turn. Believe it or not, God wrote the lead and then the rest of the story in Genesis when He told about creating man. Get your favorite version of the Bible and read Genesis 1:26-31. Answer the following questions but use *only those verses.*

1. **Who** did it?

2. **What** did he do?

3. **When** did he do it?

4. **Where** did he do it?

5. **Why** did he do it?

6. **How** did he do it?

Were you able to answer all the questions from those six verses? No, you weren't.

Those verses are God's lead, but He has to tell us more. He has to fill us in with the rest of the story. And He does. He tells it chronologically in Genesis 2:7-25. Now read that section from Genesis 2 and answer any questions that you couldn't answer before. Are there any still unanswered?

The why is still unanswered from that text. If you want to fill your readers in, you will have to do some research.

Skill 6: **No** bibliography?

Reporters and many other writers don't use a bibliography. They have to include their sources in the body of their articles. Here's a silly example of someone writing about pickles. Notice how he cites his source:

> Dill pickles are much more popular than sweet pickles. In fact, according to www.welovepickles.com, pickle lovers buy four times more dill pickles than sweet.

The words *according to* announce that a fact or a quotation is coming next. The Web site tells the readers where to look for that original information and where the writer got the information.

Here's another example of how to include your source without a bibliography:

> Police aren't the only people who can arrest someone who is breaking the law. Dr. Sassafras of the Department of Natural Resources explains that any law-enforcement conservation officer has the authority to arrest someone who is hunting without a license, catching more than the legal limit of fish, or speeding.

In this case, the writer told the readers who the information came from and where the person works. It is important to include both the person's name (*Dr. Sassafras*) and his credentials or personal identification (*of the Department of Natural Resources*) so the readers will know that this information is believable.

Below is almost the same paragraph. However, the writer is **quoting** Dr. Sassafras instead of **paraphrasing** him:

> Police aren't the only people who can arrest someone who is breaking the law. "When people hunt without a license, go over their legal limit of fish, or speed, a law-enforcement conservation officer can arrest them. He or she has full police powers," said Dr. Sassafras of the Department of Natural Resources.

The writer still included the source's name (*Dr. Sassafras*) and where he works (*of the Department of Natural Resources*). But this time he used quotation marks to indicate that he was not paraphrasing but quoting him.

These are called **attributions**. They include the source's name and identification. They also use a simple verb such as *said* or *explained*, and the verb is in the past tense. This is different than citing sources in a report or essay, which uses verbs in the present tense (*says, points out*, and so forth).

If you were writing a newspaper article on Robin Hood, your *attributions* might look like this:

- Robin Hood, author of *How I Take from the Rich and Give to the Poor,* wrote that he was doing the shire a favor.

- Robin Hood's mortal enemy, the Sheriff of Nottingham, said in his reports of the day, "He is nothing but a thieving, Saxon scoundrel."

- Little John, Robin Hood's large sidekick, said the Merry Men had nothing but good in their hearts, despite what others might have said.

- Friar Tuck, a friend of Robin Hood's, admitted this in his personal journals: "Many times, the money we steal from the lords and ladies ends up in the wrong pockets. God, help us."

- As one who lived under Robin Hood's protection for many years, Maid Marian believed that Robin Hood could do no wrong.

- "I don't know where I'd be today without the help of Robin Hood," said Bessie Essex, a poor milkmaid of that time.

- According to Robin Hood's official fan club, www.robinhoodisourman.org, rumors of violence are false.

Remember to turn off your hyperlink by right-clicking on the Web site address. Then left-click on "Hyperlink" and "Remove Hyperlink." That way, the address won't be blue in your article.

Now it's your turn. Below are some sources and their information. Put each row together to form a complete sentence so that the information becomes an attribution. Make it look like a sentence that would appear in a newspaper article. There is more than one right way to make these into sentences. Choose your own verbs and how you'll put the sentences together. Write them in the space below or on a separate piece of paper.

The Person/Site	The Identification	The Information
1. Mark Twain	author of *Roughing It*	"I was young and ignorant, and I envied my brother."
2. http://www.canalmuseum.com/	great Internet site about the Panama Canal	"A ship traveling from New York to San Francisco can save 7,872 miles using the Panama Canal instead of going around South America."
3. C.S. Lewis	author of *The Lion, the Witch, and the Wardrobe*	has credited the creation of the faun Mr. Tumnus to a dream he had in his teens
4. Maritza Ruiz	13-year-old earthquake survivor	"The ground was rolling under my feet. I felt like I was on a boat."

Skill 7: The **Assignment**

CHOOSE **ONE**:

☐ Finish the news article for which you wrote the lead on page 139 (Skill 2). Remember to use facts, not opinions. When you add the lead and the significance to the rest of the article, the total word count should be 200 to 300 words.

☐ Choose a Bible story. Write the lead, including the significance of the event. Then write the rest of the story in short paragraphs. Remember to use facts, not opinions. Word count: 200 to 300 words.

A suggested writing schedule:

Day 1   ► Decide on a Bible (or other) story. Read all you can about it to get all the facts. Take notes.

Day 2   ► Write the lead. Include the significance of the event.

Day 3   ► Write the rest of the story chronologically. Use short paragraphs.

Day 4   ► Put the lead and the story together. Proofread three times. Make a neat copy.

Remember to use the **Mistake Medic** on page 238 in **YOUR LOCKER**!

A How-to

Skill 1: Do it **This Way!**

You already know how to do many things. And you probably can take someone through the steps of how to do them.   Check everything on the list below that you know how to do:

☐ Get rid of hiccups
☐ Wash the dishes
☐ Write in calligraphy
☐ Clean your room
☐ Walk on stilts
☐ Wash the car
☐ Tell a friend about Jesus
☐ Cook macaroni and cheese
☐ Make a lamp
☐ Sew a pillowcase
☐ Swim the crawl stroke
☐ Babysit
☐ Select a new pair of shoes
☐ Collect insects
☐ Memorize Scripture
☐ Do origami
☐ Make someone laugh

☐ Plant a garden
☐ Apply first aid
☐ Play a sport
☐ Organize a camping trip
☐ Program a VCR or DVD player
☐ Style hair
☐ Make a friend
☐ Change the oil in the car
☐ Make paper hats
☐ Decorate cakes
☐ Take pictures
☐ Make jewelry
☐ Play an instrument
☐ Be a good neighbor
☐ Pack for a trip
☐ Build a birdhouse
☐ Other _____

Can you believe all the stuff you already know how to do? It's incredible!

Now it's your turn. In your lifetime, you've probably made one hundred peanut butter and jelly sandwiches. Pretend you are going to teach a younger brother or sister how to make one now.   Think about the process and write it down chronologically next to the numbers below. You might not need all the numbers, or you may want to add a few to complete your list.

1.

2.

3.

4.

5.

6.

7.

8.

9.

10.

    Read your list. Do you need to rearrange any of the steps? Did you forget any steps?   Does your list begin with "Wash your hands"? Does it end with "Clean up"?

Now it's your turn again.   Ask a parent, teacher, friend, sibling, or school partner to make the sandwich using only your list. Then stand back and watch the fun!

Making a list is essential when you write any how-to paper. It organizes your thoughts and helps you put all the steps in the right order.

Skill 2: Give me some Milk

On page 150 (Skill 1), you wrote your own list of how to make a peanut butter and jelly sandwich. Today you will read someone else's list and give it a grade.

A girl in fifth grade, a boy in sixth grade, and a boy in seventh grade made this list of how to make a peanut butter and jelly sandwich. Then they had to make the sandwich based on what they wrote. Read their list below and see how they did:

---

1. Get out the ingredients: peanut butter, bread, jelly, paper plate, knife.
2. Open the bread bag and peanut butter and jelly jars.
3. Take two slices of bread and put them on your plate.
4. Then take your butter knife, stick it in the top of the peanut butter jar, and wipe the peanut butter on the bread.
5. Next, put the same knife into the jelly and wipe the jelly onto the other piece of bread.
6. Put the two pieces of bread together, with the peanut butter piece and jelly piece of bread facing toward each other.
7. Clean up the mess.
8. Enjoy.

Now it's your turn. Answer the questions below.

1. Could you make a peanut butter and jelly sandwich from their list?

2. Add any steps they left out.

3. If you wanted to tell your readers some fun things to add to a peanut butter sandwich (other than jelly), where would you add that information?

4. Based on the order and completeness of their list, what grade would you give these students?

Skill 3: Let me show you **How**

There are two main methods of turning a list into a how-to paper. The first method is the **Essay Method**, and the second is the **Instruction Manual Method**. Both are good ways to teach someone how to do something. Today and in Skill 4, you will learn about the *Essay Method.* In Skill 5, you will learn how to do the *Instruction Manual Method.*

The Essay Method is written in essay form with an introduction, a body, and a conclusion. You are already familiar with essays, so let's see how you can use them for a how-to:

> In high school and college, a how-to is called *process writing.*

The Essay Method

1. Write a sentence or two of **introduction** to set the mood and to tell the readers what you are going to teach them.

- If you are going to teach your readers how to eat a pizza, write a sentence or two to make their mouths drool!

- If you are telling how to mow the lawn, pay attention to whether you like to mow the lawn or whether you don't. If you enjoy it, mention how fresh the grass smells or how exhilarating it is to be outdoors. If you don't like to mow, you can write a humorous paper. Mention the mosquitoes, the gasoline smell, and the fun you're missing out on while you're working.

Read this introductory paragraph.   A girl in the eighth grade wrote it to set the mood for her how-to essay on purchasing a cat:

> Are you lonely? Do you need something to cuddle up with on rainy days? I have a simple but wonderful answer: Buy a cuddly, cute, and captivating kitten! A cat's feline instincts provide a lovable feeling that will warm you up on wintry days. Read on to find out how to purchase a faithful friend.

She is obviously in favor of buying cats, and it shows!

2. **List items** or ingredients the readers will need.   Depending on what you are teaching, this step may not be necessary.

3. Go **step by step** chronologically. Avoid skipping around. It's confusing!

4. **Be clear** in your instructions.

- Work to make your instructions easy to understand. Avoid using complicated words and sentences.

- Be aware of who your audience is. Are you teaching a younger sibling? Are you teaching your peers? A parent? Does your audience already know something about the subject? Each of these will need different wording so the readers can understand the process clearly.

There are four more steps to turning a list into a how-to essay. In Skill 4 you will learn the remaining four steps.

Now it's your turn. Choose something you know how to do. Then decide who your audience is. Write an introductory paragraph to set the mood for your how-to essay. Is it cozy, serious, humorous, or practical? Let your readers know in the first paragraph what to expect. Use the rest of this page.

I am going to teach the readers how to _____

My audience is _____

INTRODUCTORY PARAGRAPH:

Skill 4: The **Essay Method** (continued)

On pages 152 and 153 (Skill 3), you learned the first four steps to changing a how-to list into a how-to essay. Today you will learn the last four steps.

Now it's your turn. From memory, write the first four steps. After you have written all that you can remember, you may turn back to pages 152 and 153 (Skill 3) to find the steps you didn't remember.

1.

2.

3.

4.

The Essay Method (continued)

5. **Use transition words** and phrases between the steps. This leads the readers from one step to another very easily. Read the transition words and phrases in the list below. Can you think of others?

First	Then	After that
Next	Second	Now
Begin by	When you have done	Finally
Then you are ready to	Last	Once you have

6. Include **charts or pictures** if necessary. In complicated instructions, sometimes only a chart or picture will help the readers know how to do the next step.

7. **Define** any jargon (special terms). Notice how *jargon* was neatly defined for you in the parentheses. Make sure your readers understand the special terms that apply to your topic, especially if you know that your audience is unfamiliar with the topic. Read the sentence below and determine what might be wrong:

Now that you have all your equipment, let's go fly-fishing.

An expert fisherman will know exactly what you mean by *fly-fishing*. But many other people won't know. Maybe you have just invited readers to fish for buzzing flies! Define your terms! (And know your audience!)

8. Write a sentence or two of **conclusion** to tell the readers what to do once they've made the item or finished the project.

- Did you just teach your readers how to build a birdhouse? Then encourage them to hang it up, watch for new occupants, and buy a bird book to identify their new friends.

- Was your paper on how to make chocolate chip cookies? Then invite your readers to enjoy the warm cookies with a glass of cold milk.

Read the concluding paragraph below. The same eighth-grade girl who wrote the introduction on how to purchase a cat wrote this. She shows the readers how to enjoy the new cat:

Now that you have a cute little feline, the best time to enjoy her is on a windy night in your living room with a roaring fire. Cats are also quite good for cleaning up leftover tuna or salmon juice as well as providing lots of entertainment. I also recommend strongly that you repeat these steps and purchase *another* cozy, clean, and charming kitten.

Here are all the steps again but without any breaks:

1. **Write an introduction** to set the mood and to tell readers what you are going to teach them.

2. **List items** or ingredients the readers will need.

3. Go **step by step** chronologically.

4. **Be clear** in your instructions.

5. **Use transition words** and phrases between the steps.

6. Include **charts or pictures** if necessary.

7. **Define** any jargon.

8. **Write a conclusion** to tell readers what to do once they're finished.

> Process writing can be used anywhere, even in *stories*. Laura Ingalls Wilder used it in the Little House series every time she wrote how Pa made something.

Now it's your turn. Below is a how-to essay of 196 words written by a sixth-grade boy. Circle his (list of ingredients.) Underline his transition words and phrases. Put numbers next to his steps; are they chronological? Put an arrow (→) next to the sentence in which he tells you how to use your chalk.

How to Make Homemade Chalk

You will need the following items: an empty toilet paper tube, 1¼ cups plaster of Paris, waxed paper, a disposable container (such as a 15 oz. or larger margarine tub), a plastic spoon, ½ cup water, and, finally, tempera paint.

First, line the inside of your toilet paper tube with waxed paper and set the tube upright on another sheet of waxed paper. Next, make the plaster. Mix together the water and plaster of Paris in the disposable container. When the mixture is smooth, add several spoonfuls of paint until you get the color you like. (I used six spoonfuls of yellow paint and three spoonfuls of red paint to make the color orange.) After you've completed that, use a plastic spoon to put the plaster in the tube. Gently tap the tube to remove any air bubbles.

When you are done, throw away the container and the spoon. Be careful not to get any plaster down your sink because it will dry and clog up your pipes!

After twenty-four hours, the plaster should be dry. Carefully peel away the tube from the chalk and take the chalk out of the waxed paper. Have fun drawing!

---

1. Reread the list on the previous page. Does this writer leave out anything?

2. What does he do well?

3. Based on what you know about a how-to, what grade would you give him?

Skill 5: Where's the **Instruction Manual?**

Have you bought anything new lately? A game? A CD player? A camera? When you buy something new, you often get an instruction manual with it. It tells you how to play the game, how to program the CD player, or how to take the best pictures.

Instruction manuals are written as lists. The buyer wants to learn quickly how to do something, and a list is just the thing to help him do that. Today you will learn the Instruction Manual Method for turning your list into something someone can use.

The Instruction Manual Method

1. **List items** or ingredients the readers will need.

2. Go **step by step** chronologically, using numbers.

3. **Be clear** in your instructions.

4. **Use transition words** and phrases between the steps, but only if necessary.

5. Include **charts or pictures** if necessary.

6. **Define** any jargon.

7. Use the **present tense** and **imperative** sentences.

Does this list look familiar? It should. It is almost the same list from the Essay Method but without the introduction and conclusion paragraphs. You simply use numbers instead of paragraphs for the steps.

There is one new item on the list, though. Number seven explains that you begin each sentence with a verb in the present tense and that all of your sentences are imperative. Imperative sentences are commands: *Wash your hands, Clean your room, Bite the dog,* and *Define any jargon.* The subject of an imperative sentence is always an understood *You.*

Notice that the Instruction Manual Method list above contains only imperative sentences. Also, each sentence begins with a verb in the present tense: *list, go, be, use, include, define,* and *use.* This makes the list easy to understand and easy to follow.

By now you have noticed that the above Instruction Manual Method list was written using the Instruction Manual Method!

Now it's your turn. Read the how-to list below. A boy in the fifth grade wrote it using the Instruction Manual Method. <u>Underline</u> his verbs. Notice their tense and their position.

Yummy Stuff

1. Wash your hands before doing anything.
2. Preheat oven to 350 degrees.
3. Get out the following:
   1 medium mixing bowl
   1 liquid measuring cup
   1 rubber spatula
   1 electric mixer
4. Gather your ingredients:
   1 18.5 oz. dry cake mix, any flavor
   1 1/3 cups water
   1/3 cup vegetable oil
   2 large eggs
5. Pour dry cake mix from package into mixing bowl.
6. Measure and pour 1 1/3 cups water and 1/3 cup oil into mixing bowl.
7. Add eggs one at a time to the mixture.
8. Turn electric mixer on and beat mixture at low speed until moistened (about 30 seconds). Then continue beating on medium speed for 2 more minutes.
9. Pour mixture into 2 8" square pans, greased and lightly floured.
10. Bake in preheated oven for 33-36 minutes or until toothpick comes out clean.
11. Ice cake when completely cool.
12. Cut and enjoy.

Skill 6: The **Assignment**

CHOOSE **ONE**:

☐ Write a how-to in the Essay Method. Use 100 to 300 words. Include pictures or charts if necessary.

☐ Write a how-to in the Instruction Manual Method. Use 100 to 300 words. Include pictures or charts if necessary.

A suggested writing schedule:

Day 1   ↪ Decide what you want to teach. Choose your audience. Write your list of steps.

Days 2-3   ↪ Decide on your method. Write your paper.

Day 4   ↪ Reread to make sure your steps are in the right order and you have not forgotten any steps. Create any charts or pictures you may need.

Day 5   ↪ Proofread three separate times for mistakes. Make a neat copy.

Remember to use the **Mistake Medic** on page 238 in **YOUR LOCKER**!

Compare and Contrast

Skill 1: What's the Big Deal?

For today's lesson you will need to **get one of the following sets** of things:

- A box of facial tissues and a cloth handkerchief
- A book and a movie video or DVD (of the same book, if that's possible)
- A hymnal and a praise chorus book
- A math or science textbook and crayons or paints (to represent art classes)
- A pine branch and a piece of an imitation pine (or Christmas) tree
- A can of soda (pop) and bottled water
- A pen and a pencil
- A box of raisins and a can of fruit

Put the two items you chose in front of you and think about them. You will compare them: What are their **similarities**? You will also contrast them: What are their **differences**?

In very plain English, that is what a **compare-and-contrast** assignment is all about—looking at two things or two people and thinking about their *similarities* and *differences*.

Let's say, for example, that you chose the pine branch/piece of imitation pine tree for your set. The pine branch, by the way, represents a real evergreen Christmas tree, and the imitation pine branch represents an imitation Christmas tree. What are the similarities between a real Christmas tree and an imitation

Christmas tree?   What are the differences?   Read the lists below to see some ideas.

REAL TREE VERSUS IMITATION TREE FOR CHRISTMAS

SIMILARITIES

- They're both green.
- They both hold many ornaments.
- They both can be lit up.
- They both help celebrate Christmas.
- They both tower above presents.
- They both take up a lot of space.
- They both look nice when decorated.

DIFFERENCES (Real in red/imitation in green)

- Smells nice/has no scent
- Buy a new one every year/use the same one year after year
- Irregular limbs/nice, even limbs
- Throw it away/keep it from year to year
- Needles to clean up/no needles to vacuum

Now it's your turn.   Using the set of items you chose on page 161, make your own lists of similarities and differences.

SET of ITEMS: _____

SIMILARITIES   DIFFERENCES

Skill 2: Which is **Better?**

Now that you have made a list of similarities and differences, you have a choice to make—and I don't think it will be too difficult.
Choose which one of the two items *you like better:*

- Which one would you rather use: a disposable facial tissue or a reusable handkerchief? Why?
- Which one would you rather do: read a book or watch the movie based on the book? Why?
- Which one would you rather sing: hymns or praise choruses? Why?
- Which class would you rather take: a math or science class, or an art class? Why?

I'm sure you have the idea by now. You get to choose which one you like better, and you get to say why.

Now it's your turn. Using the set you chose and the lists you wrote on page 162 (Skill 1), write which item of the two you prefer. Then write why. Brainstorm five reasons.

I prefer _____

because…

1.

2.

3.

4.

5.

Skill 3: **Imitate** me

The following paragraph of 96 words is from *Anne's House of Dreams* by L. M. Montgomery. She is comparing and contrasting two things: the woods and the sea. After you read the paragraph, read the lists of similarities and differences between the woods and the sea.

The woods are never solitary—they are full of whispering, beckoning, friendly life. But the sea is a mighty soul, forever moaning of some great, unshareable[1] sorrow, which shuts it up into itself for all eternity. We can never pierce its infinite mystery—we may only wander, awed and spell-bound, on the outer fringe of it. The woods call to us with a hundred voices, but the sea has one only—a mighty voice that drowns our souls in its majestic music. The woods are human, but the sea is of the company of the archangels.[2]

SIMILARITIES

- Both are elements of nature.
- Both meet at the shore.
- Both have a voice.

DIFFERENCES (woods/sea)

- The woods are friendly./The sea is solitary and sorrowful.
- We can enter the woods./We can never enter the sea and know its secrets.
- The woods have a hundred voices./The sea has only one.
- The woods are of the earth (human)./The sea is heavenly.

Now it's your turn. Answer these questions below. Then go to the next page.

1. Which does the author like better: the woods or the sea? _____

2. Which do you like best? Why? _____

_____

_____

[1] This is an old way to spell "unsharable."
[2] L. M. Montgomery, *Anne's House of Dreams* (New York: Bantam Books, 1998), 54.

3. Which does she mention first? _____

4. Which does she mention last? _____

There are five sentences in the paragraph from *Anne's House of Dreams*. Using the numbers below to represent each sentence, put the word *woods* or *sea* next to each number. Here's how:

If the author wrote about the woods in sentence one, you will put *woods* next to #1. If she wrote about the sea in sentence one, you will put *sea* next to #1. If she wrote about both of them in any sentence, you will write both words and put them in the order you find them in the original sentence. Feel free to use different colors to keep the woods and the sea distinct.

1.

2.

3.

4.

5.

Skill 4: A **Pattern** to **Follow**

Now you have a pattern to imitate if you are writing one paragraph.

- Lucy Montgomery's pattern of woods and sea is very specific in each sentence:

  1. woods   (don't like as much)
  2. sea   (like)
  3. sea   (like)
  4. woods, sea   (don't like as much, like)
  5. woods, sea   (don't like as much, like)

- Sentence 1 describes the woods.
- Sentences 2 and 3 describe the sea.
- Sentences 4 and 5 contrast the woods and the sea in each sentence, with the sea coming out as the winner.

Your five sentences will do the same thing with your own set of items. Your first sentence will talk about the thing you didn't like as much. The last part of your last sentence will be about the thing you liked best. If you prefer a real Christmas tree to an imitation one, your sentences will use this pattern:

  1. imitation   (don't like as much)
  2. real   (like)
  3. real   (like)
  4. imitation, real   (don't like as much, like)
  5. imitation, real   (don't like as much, like)

What will be in your sentences? The stuff from the lists you made on page 162 (Skill 1) and some of the pleasant things you prefer from page 163 (Skill 2).

Now it's your turn. Use the set of items you chose on pages 161 and 162 (Skill 1). Fill in your items below, using Lucy Montgomery's pattern. Begin with the item that you don't like as much. End with the item that you do like. Numbers four and five will contain two items each.

1.   4.

2.   5.

3.

Now it's your turn again. In the space below, write a compare-and-contrast paragraph for your set of items. You will need five sentences and about 100 words, using the pattern L. M. Montgomery used.

Skill 5: **Cats** and **Dogs**

You have a pattern to use if you ever want to write a compare-and-contrast paragraph again. But what if you have to write a *whole paper* comparing and contrasting two governments, two presidents, or two characters from a novel?

Never fear. Help is near.

Read "My New Pet," an opinion paper below of 250 words about cats. It should look familiar. You read it in "Opinions—You've Got Them!" When you compare it to "Cats Win" (395 words) on the next page, you will notice that the points are exactly the same in both: Cats are clean, smart, and polite. In fact, the very same words about cats appear in the bodies of "My New Pet" and "Cats Win."

In "Cats Win," however, the writer added words and sentences about dogs, comparing and contrasting cats to dogs so that cats will seem much better in the end. "My New Pet" is not a compare-and-contrast paper. It appears here to show you how to use the body of an opinion paper to begin one, though. The colors are to highlight the parts about cats and the parts about dogs.

My New Pet

When my mom said I could have a pet, I went to the pet store to look at all the animals. Which one did I choose? I saw the cute gerbils and hamsters scurrying in their cages. I listened to the canaries, parakeets, and finches singing. I watched the three fuzzy puppies playing with a ball. But when I came to the kitten cage, I knew what I wanted.

Cats are clean. They are constantly licking themselves to remove burrs, dirt, and unpleasant smells. Cats can be trained to use a kitty litter box, making it easy to clean up after them.

Cats are smart. They cover up their messes. And if you happen to miss a day feeding your cats, it is only a small problem to them. They know how to find mice, moles, small rabbits, and even moths for their meals.

Cats are polite. They quietly walk through the house, minding their own business. They are not fussy, and they have manners.

I chose a white and butterscotch kitten, and I named her Sundae. Mom bought a scratching post so Sundae would have a safe place to sharpen her claws. I bought a little ball with a bell inside it so Sundae could have something to play with. She's the cutest thing! She's a fluffy ball of fur. I loved having a kitten so much that I went back the next day and bought Chocolate, her sister. Now I have two pets, and I love them both!

Cats Win

Sloppy drool on the windows, sharp barking waking you up at night, and huge, muddy paws getting your clothes dirty as he jumps uncontrollably on you—or a self-washing, quiet bundle of warm fur. Which would you rather have? For me, it is no contest. I prefer the cat.

Cats are clean. They are constantly licking themselves to remove burrs, dirt, and unpleasant smells. Cats can be trained to use a kitty litter box, making it easy to clean up after them. Not so with dogs, who require us to bathe them after they've romped through the muddy, moldy pond water or through the neighbor's rotted, decayed, week-old garbage. Can you imagine dogs ever using a doggy litter box? No. We have to open the doors for them whenever they feel the urge, and then we have to clean up after them before our next volleyball game. They are lacking the instinct and the intelligence to cover up their mess.

Cats are smart. They cover up their messes. And if you happen to miss a day feeding your cats, it is only a small problem to them. They know how to find mice, moles, small rabbits, and even moths for their meals. A dog, on the other hand, may make large holes in your yard looking for moles, but he has no intention of eating them if he ever finds them. He requires huge, heavy bags of food, and he needs a leash to keep him from playing with skunks.

Cats are polite. They don't jump up on you and demand your attention. Cats don't slobber in your face and lick you with giant, bad-smelling tongues. They quietly walk through the house, minding their own business. They are not fussy, and they have manners.

Yes, they are both four-footed, furry animals. And, yes, they are both pets. But that's where the similarities end. Our neighbor's heavy dog has jumped up on me with muddy paws. He constantly licks my hands as though they were meat on a stick. He barks at small animals in the middle of the night. And he even steals our cats' empty food dishes and deposits them anywhere he pleases. Our cats have never done any of these rude things to any of our neighbors, and they never will. Cats can live at my house for as long as they wish.

These sentences are blue because they are referring to doggy behavior (jumping, slobbering, etc.).

You will be clever enough to notice that "Cats Win" shows more differences (contrasts) than similarities (comparisons). In order to show which of two things is better, you will often write more differences than similarities.

A few sentences are written about cats for each point and then a few sentences about dogs. This gives the readers a smoother experience and avoids the ping-pong effect. Here is an example of the ping-pong effect:

Cats cover up their messes. Dogs don't. Cats know how to find moles to eat. Dogs know how to find moles, but they won't eat them. Cats mind their own business. Dogs jump on you.

You want to avoid going back and forth like that for every sentence. Your readers will get dizzy!

The introductions and conclusions for both papers are different. "My New Pet" is an opinion paper and begins and ends with a story. "Cats Win" is a compare-and-contrast paper and uses interesting statements in its introduction and conclusion to highlight differences between dogs and cats.

In an introduction for your compare-and-contrast paper, say something that will give a hint to the readers that you are comparing and contrasting two things and that one of them is the better one.

There are many right ways to write a compare-and-contrast paper. <u>Try this method</u>: When you begin your own compare and contrast paper, write the reasons and the body as though you were writing an opinion paper. Then go back and fill in the contrasting parts (the differences). This is what the writer of "Cats Win" did. The body of the opinion paper gives you a form upon which to hang some "clothes" (the differences) later.

Now it's your turn.   Answer the questions below.

1. Write the sentence that is the thesis statement in "Cats Win":

2. List the similarities between cats and dogs (according to the writer). Then list the differences.

<u>SIMILARITIES</u>   <u>DIFFERENCES</u>

3. Do you agree with the writer of "Cats Win"? If not, state why.

Skill 6: A useful Tool

Now it's your turn. A seventh-grade boy wrote this persuasive paper of 322 words to compare and contrast his two dogs. He used "Cats Win" as his example. In "The Best Dog in the World," he wants to convince readers that one of his dogs is better than the other. The colors are to show you which parts are of Beau and which are of Winnie. Read his paper and answer the questions afterward.

The Best Dog in the World

One scary, stormy night, I was sleeping downstairs, accompanied by my two canine friends, Winnie in the corner and Beau to my side. Beau, the wise, wide-eyed, wonderful dog, lay next to me trying to protect me, while Winnie, on the other hand, cowardly sat in the corner trying to stay safe. So which would you prefer: the scared, self-centered dog or the loyal, loving guard dog? For me the choice is obvious. I'd choose Beau.

Beau is very kind. He doesn't bark at friends when they pull into our driveway. Patiently Beau waits for food. Beau loves to spend time with everyone. This very kind and loving dog could almost be a human being by the way he acts.

Beau can do many tricks. He can balance a treat on his snout and then catch it, and he can perform basic tricks like sit, shake, speak, stay, come, and roll over. And we must not forget playing fetch, which is his favorite. Winnie, on the other hand, won't fetch the toy that you fling, so you're stuck having to go chase it down. Also, if you try to put a treat on Winnie's nose, she'll just bite you before you can pull your hand back.

Beau is an obedient dog. He doesn't run off in the middle of the night. If you're trying to tie your shoes on the front porch, Beau will leave if you tell him to, but Winnie will go right on annoying you. When the dogs are barking, Beau will stop when told, even if Winnie does not.

Although Winnie has good looks, many people believe in brains over beauty. Winnie may look cute and innocent, but don't let her fool you. She's really just waiting for you to feel sorry for her and give her a treat. If I had to make a choice between Winnie and Beau, in the end, the winner would be Beau.

1. Which dog does he mention first? _____

2. Which dog does he mention last? _____

3. Which does he like more? _____

4. What are his three points, which become areas of contrast for the two dogs?

    •

    •

    •

5. In paragraph two, what does he leave out? _____

_____

6. Which dog would you rather have? _____

7. Based on your knowledge of compare-and-contrast papers, what grade would you give this student? _____

Compare and contrast is a handy tool. You will use it in many kinds of writing. Here are a few examples:

→ **Persuasion:** Compare and contrast two candy bars to show the readers that they should buy one instead of the other.
→ **Exposition:** Compare and contrast two explorers and their treatment of indigenous people (the people who lived there before the explorers arrived).
→ **Description:** Compare and contrast two things from nature to show which one is nicer or to set a mood.
→ **Narration:** Compare and contrast two people to show which one is the better person.

Skill 7: The **Assignment**

If you are a beginning writer:

➡ Choose two elements of nature, two people, or two objects. Compare and contrast them and show which one you prefer, using the five-sentence pattern you learned. Word count: approximately 100 words.

Day 1 ➥ Decide on your topic. Make lists of similarities and differences. Choose which one you like best. Make a list of the key words for the five sentences.

Day 2 ➥ Write your five sentences and proofread. Make a neat copy.

If you are an experienced writer:

➡ Choose a set of items, people, places, events, or anything else to compare and contrast. Use "Cats Win" as your writing example. Word count: at least 300 words.

Day 1 ➥ Decide on your topic. List the similarities and differences. Research if needed. Decide which of the set is the best.

Days 2-3 ➥ Write the body of your paper as you would for an opinion paper. Use three separate points, which will become areas of contrast for you. Then add the contrast (differences).

Day 4 ➥ Write the introduction and conclusion.

Day 5 ➥ Proofread three separate times for mistakes. Make a neat copy.

Remember to use the **Mistake Medic** on page 238 in **YOUR LOCKER!**

A Description

Skill 1: That's **Short!**

News flash: A good description can be as short as one word. It's true. Incredible but true.

That one word might be an **adjective**—a word used to describe or modify a noun—or a **noun** itself. Consider the following sentence:

> She held a bird in her hands.

That sentence raises more questions than it answers. What kind of bird was it? How big? How small? What color? Dead? Alive? Take a look at the following sentences to see how one small word (an *adjective* or a specific *noun*) can change everything:

> She held a <u>trembling</u> bird in her hands.
> She held a <u>baby</u> bird in her hands.
> She held an <u>owlet</u> in her hands.
> She held a <u>parrot</u> in her hands.
> She held a <u>hungry</u> bird in her hands.
> She held a <u>screeching</u> bird in her hands.
> She held a <u>dying</u> bird in her hands.

Just one little word (adjective or noun) can change the whole meaning and feel of the sentence. You can do the same thing with her hands too:

She held a trembling bird in her <u>chapped</u> hands.
She held a baby bird in her <u>competent</u> hands.
She held an owlet in her <u>muddy</u> hands.

Now it's your turn. Choose specific adjectives and nouns to make these sentences come alive.

<u>Examples:</u>

He drove his <u>tractor</u> like a <u>race-car</u> driver.
He drove his <u>Jaguar</u> like an <u>old</u> man.

1. He drove his _____ like a(n) _____ man.

2. The _____ broke a window on the _____ house.

3. The _____ girl dived into the _____ pool.

4. The _____ garden was filled with _____.

Skill 2: Canary? **Peacock?** Parrot?

Now it's your turn.   Pretend there are 19 birds in the room with you. Your job is to describe one of them so well that the reader can easily pick out which bird you are describing. You are *not* allowed to tell the type of bird! Remember to use specific adjectives and nouns in your description. You may use this page or a separate piece of paper.

Word count: under 75 words.

(Note: If writing about a bird is uninspiring to you, imagine another group of 19 animals and write about one of them.)

Skill 3: Still **One Word!**

You have seen how a specific adjective or noun can light up a sentence. So can a **powerful verb.** Look at this bland sentence:

The man came into the room.

That sentence does nothing for the reader. It says nothing about how the man came into the room. Unless you have a vivid imagination, you can't picture him coming into the room because the writer didn't tell you how the man came into the room. It's the writer's job to make word pictures for the reader.

Look at the interesting things that happen when you change the *verb* (we're concentrating on the verb now, not an adjective for the man):

The man <u>shot</u> into the room.
The man <u>limped</u> into the room.
The man <u>slithered</u> into the room.

Each new verb is powerful and specific, creating a better word picture. It tells you exactly how the man came into the room, and it tells you something about the man. In the first sentence, he was in a hurry; in the second, he could be hurt; and in the third, you might get a creepy feeling about him because he *slithered*, something a snake does.

A specific verb is always more powerful than an adverb.

Notice that *The man <u>shot</u> into the room* is more powerful than *The man <u>came</u> into the room <u>quickly</u>.* *The man <u>slithered</u> into the room* is more powerful than *The man <u>came</u> into the room <u>slyly</u>.* Why? *Quickly* and *slyly* are adverbs. They don't hit as hard. Whenever possible, use a powerful and specific verb instead of an adverb.

Now it's your turn. Think of powerful and specific verbs to tell the reader how the man came into the room. Fill in the blanks.

The man _____ into the room.

The man _____ into the room.

The man _____ into the room.

The man _____ into the room.

The man _____ into the room.

The man _____ into the room.

Think about this: You've been using verbs to describe how a *man* came into a room. Would you use different verbs for a woman? A girl? A toddler? Probably. Write four powerful and specific verbs to describe how a *woman* can come into a room.

1.
2.
3.
4.

Now write four powerful and specific verbs to describe how a *girl* might come into a room.

1.
2.
3.
4.

Some of the verbs can be the same for either gender. A man *or* a woman can charge into a room, but if a grown man skips into a room, we had better know why!

You can do the same thing with the verb *said,* which has many synonyms. Using a thesaurus (a special book that lists synonyms) will give you ideas. Instead of writing *he said softly*, which uses an adverb, write *he whispered.* It is clearer and more specific.

What are some other specific verbs you can use for *said*? Yelled? Whined? Announced? In the space below, write four more.

Skill 4: I'm **Yawning!**

Now it's your turn.   The following paragraph contains 127 words of dullness. It lacks specific adjectives and nouns. It also lacks powerful verbs. Write your version of it on a separate piece of paper. Change anything you need to in order to make this lackluster paragraph interesting. Make this story come alive! Make it sparkle!

We looked out the kitchen window and saw a tornado coming toward us. It kept coming and coming. It was very fast. We picked up our little brother and went to the truck. Then we got into the truck. We were going to outrun the tornado. We were very scared. Then we remembered that we are not supposed to outrun a tornado. We decided to hide in the closet under the stairs. We went there with our little brother. Then we shut the closet door. It was very scary. When we heard a big, scary noise, the house began to shake. Suddenly, it was very quiet. We left the closet and looked at our house. The kitchen was gone. Now I won't have to wash the dishes!

A suggested writing schedule:

Day 1   ⇨ Rewrite the paragraph.

Day 2   ⇨ Proofread three times. Make a neat copy.

Remember to use the **Mistake Medic** on page 238 in **YOUR LOCKER!**

Skill 5: She sings **Like** a **Bird!**

You are probably familiar with the terms **simile (sim' uh lee)** and **metaphor.** Today you will review the *simile*. In Skill 6, you will review the *metaphor*.

A **simile** compares two things for the purpose of giving one of them more meaning. It uses the words *like* or *as*. The Bible is loaded with great similes:

- Samaria and its king will float away **like** a twig on the surface of the waters (Hosea 10:7 NIV).

- His head and hair were white **like** wool, **as** white **as** snow, and his eyes were **like** blazing fire. His feet were **like** bronze glowing in a furnace, and his voice was **like** the sound of rushing waters (Revelation 1:14-15).

- A word aptly spoken is **like** apples of gold in settings of silver (Proverbs 25:11).

Now it's your turn. Fill in the blanks of these similes. Try not to write the obvious words. Be creative.

She is as smart as a(n) _____.

It was quick like a(n) _____.

The soldier was as stubborn as a(n)_____.

The smell was as strong as a(n) _____.

The room was as quiet as a(n) _____.

Taking a vacation is like _____.

_____.

Doing homework is like _____

_____.

> Sometimes the words *like* and *as* have other jobs to do and are not signaling a simile. To make sure you are reading a simile, check to see if two things are being compared to each other.

Skill 6: A Word **Picture**

A **metaphor** compares two things to make one of them more meaningful, but it does <u>not</u> use the words *like* or *as*. The Bible is full of wonderful *metaphors:*

Do you see how comparing God's Word to a lamp and a light helps us understand its purpose in our lives?

- I will remove from you your heart **of stone** and give you a heart of flesh (Ezekiel 36:26b).

- Your word is **a lamp to my feet** and a **light for my path** (Psalm 119:105).

- I think it is right to refresh your memory as long as I live in **the tent** of this body (2 Peter 1:13).

Why would Peter call his body a tent? Because his body was only a temporary place to live, and it was wearing out (getting old), just like a tent.

Here is a metaphor written by Henry David Thoreau on June 17, 1854:

The dewy cobwebs are very thick this morning, **little napkins of the fairies spread on the grass.**

That is a beautiful word picture of how cobwebs look in the early morning. Have you ever seen them like that in the grass?

Now it's your turn. There are many metaphors in well-written books. Use the Bible or a fiction book you are reading for school. Find two metaphors and write them in the space below.

1.

2.

Skill 7: What's **Out There?**

People who write good descriptions pay attention to detail. The famous fictional detective Sherlock Holmes once said that we often *see*, but we don't *observe*. For example, how many windows—without looking—are on the front of your house or school? Write the number in this blank: _____. The next time you get the chance, look at the front of your house or school and write the number of windows you see: _____. Are the numbers the same? How observant were you?

It is important to pay attention to your senses. You remember them from science class: sight, taste, hearing, smell, and touch. A good writer will incorporate some of these senses into his descriptions. That way the reader can experience the sense too.

Now it's your turn. Choose a place to sit. Get comfortable. It can be outside, in your room, in your basement, in a corner, next to a window, at your desk—anywhere. For the next ten minutes, list all the sensory things you experience. Be specific. If you see a tree, don't write down *tree*. Write *maple* or *ancient live oak* or, at the very least, *a bushy tree with little lavender buds*.

> Taking a walk through the woods or down a busy street is a great way to gather sensory details.

1. Sight:

2. Taste:

3. Hearing:

4. Smell:

5. Touch:

Skill 8: A **Visitor**

On page 183 (Skill 7), you listed sensory experiences for a particular place. Today you will use your sensory information to write about that place so that someone can visit it. Who is the visitor? That's up to you.

Choose a fictional character from a book you've read or a movie you've seen. You will put that character into the place you observed. Who is your character? Write his or her name in the blank:

Fictional character: _____

Now it's your turn. With your fictional character in mind, write a paragraph describing the place you visited on page 183. Let your character walk into the place and experience what you experienced there.

Will the character like the place? Then point out the pleasant things about it.

A good writer will help the reader feel what the character is experiencing.

Will the character be uncomfortable there? Then write about the things that will make him or her uncomfortable.

Write your paragraph on a separate piece of paper. Remember to use the sensory information you've already gathered. Add more, if necessary.

Word count: at least 100 words.

A suggested writing schedule:

Day 1   ➤ Write your character into a place. Describe the place and your character's reaction to it.

Day 2   ➤ Proofread three times. Make a neat copy.

Remember to use the **Mistake Medic** on page 238 in **YOUR LOCKER!**

Skill 9: Not just a **Box**

You probably spend most of your days in rooms. In books, many things happen in rooms too. A good writer will not only put the characters in the room but will also try to put the reader in the room. How will she do that? By using sensory details like the ones you recorded earlier.

A boy in the sixth grade wrote the following 109 words about a room:

Orchestra Rehearsal

Every Sunday, I come into the room at Butler University. When I get there, only one or two people are there. I hear all the clanking and screeching of music stands getting set up and chairs getting moved into position. Soon I see more people come in and hear the clicks of their cases as they open them. I can feel my body shivering like a cat shaking in the strong wind because the flute is hitting a screeching high note. Mrs. Goldman is a ballerina dancing on the conducting platform. When we leave, I say goodbye to all my friends and hop into the van like a kangaroo.

Now it's your turn.   Answer the questions.
1. Which sense does he use the most? _____
2. What other senses does he use? _____
3. <u>Underline</u> his two similes.
4. Put an X next to his metaphor.
5. Can you see his orchestra room in your mind's eye? _____

Now it's your turn again. Describe a room. Write about a room you are familiar with or make one up. Use a separate piece of paper. Word count: at least 100 words.
1. Use as many senses as you can.
2. Use one simile or one metaphor.
3. Use specific nouns and adjectives and powerful verbs.

A suggested writing schedule:

Day 1   ☐ Decide on a real or imaginary place. Using your
                 descriptive skills (including senses), write about it.

Day 2   ☐ Proofread three times. Make a neat copy.

Remember to use the **Mistake Medic** on page 238 in **YOUR LOCKER!**

Skill 10: Give me a **Direction**

Even when writers use specific nouns, strong verbs, similes, metaphors, and many senses, they have to find a way to organize their descriptions. How do they do it? They use a **spatial description**.

Try describing a baseball from the inside out. How about describing a book from its cover to its contents (outside to inside)?

A *spatial description—*where things are—is a way of organizing the information for the reader so he can see it clearly. Will you describe a room from left to right? From top to bottom? From closest to the door to the farthest wall?

You may also use this technique to describe a person. Read this description (113 words) of a man, written by a boy in the eighth grade. Are you interested in the man he describes?

> As I walked through the forest, I suddenly stopped. The forest cleared at that point, and in that clearing there stood a cabin. In front of the cabin stood a man, his hair calm and neat, his face concentrated on his work. He was clad in a plaid shirt and jeans, and his arms, thick with muscles, looked like the arms of a great black bear. His legs were as nimble and quick as a mountain goat's yet strong enough to carry the largest of loads. As he finished working on the deerskin, he looked up and, for the first time, saw me. His piercing gaze seemed to ask, "Where have you been?"

Now it's your turn. Answer the questions.

1. What is the direction of the spatial description? _____

2. <u>Underline</u> the two similes he used to describe the man.

Here is a paragraph about a girl, written by a girl in the eighth grade. She used 111 words. Would you like to meet the girl with the braids?

> Her traditional German braids, like twin vines, hung, swung, and danced according to her movements. Clear, sharp, fairy-tale blue eyes sparkled from her oval face. She was slender and exceptionally tall for her age. Her denim overalls were soaked at the knees, reminding me of the damp leaves plastering the forest floor. But before I could think what had happened to her, she skipped down the path, chatting much of the time. Then—what was that? She must have caught the strange sound, too. Leaping, climbing, and scrambling, she hurried toward it with great delight. Even though her laughter grew fainter and fainter, her captivating presence still hung in the air.

Now it's your turn again. Answer the questions.

1. What do you think she heard in the forest? _____

2. What kind of a girl is she? _____

_____

3. What direction is the spatial description? _____

4. <u>Underline</u> her simile.

5. **Assonance** is repeating a vowel sound on the insides of words in a row. Edgar Allan Poe uses *assonance* in his poem "The Bells": "m<u>o</u>lten-g<u>o</u>lden n<u>o</u>tes." Where does the writer of the paragraph about the girl use assonance?

_____

Skill 11: Who's **That?**

Read the following paragraph (131 words). What do you think of the girl?

Her black leather boots were scuffed and covered with mud—or worse. The heavy, sharp odor of a pig barn stung my eyes and made them water. Thick burrs imbedded themselves in her denim jeans, which looked as if they'd been dragged back and forth across barbed wire from the knees down. Bloody scratches showed beneath the rips. As she bent to hide them from me, steam rose from the back of her rain-soaked jacket like morning fog on the river. I tried to brush some hay from her back and her hair, but she pushed my hand aside with her muddy hand and stopped me with her cool, clear eyes. Even the hair plastered to her face could not dim those eyes. Boy, was I glad to see her again!

Now it's your turn. Answer the questions.

1. In what direction is the description? _____

2. Do you know what color her hair and eyes are? _____

3. Underline the simile.

4. What are your impressions of this person? _____

_____

5. What senses were used?

_____

Now it's your turn again. Write a paragraph describing a person. Decide on a direction in which to describe your person: head to foot, left to right, outside to inside (from looks to character), etc. Use at least one simile or metaphor.
    Include specific adjectives and nouns, powerful verbs, and a few senses.
    Word count: at least 100 words.

A suggested writing schedule:

Day 1   ❑ Describe a person. Use all of your descriptive skills plus a spatial description.

Day 2   ❑ Proofread three times. Make a neat copy.

Remember to use the **Mistake Medic** on page 238 in **YOUR LOCKER**!

Skill 12: You won't believe what's **In There!**

Read this paragraph from *The Phantom Tollbooth*, written by Norton Juster. The book contains a bored kid, a tollbooth that shows up out of nowhere, and a lot of word fun. In this paragraph, Milo (the bored kid) has just stepped into the marketplace in Dictionopolis:

> Milo could see crowds of people pushing and shouting their way among the stalls, buying and selling, trading and bargaining. Huge wooden-wheeled carts streamed into the market square from the orchards, and long caravans bound for the four corners of the kingdom made ready to leave. Sacks and boxes were piled high waiting to be delivered to the ships that sailed the Sea of Knowledge, and off to one side a group of minstrels sang songs to the delight of those either too young or too old to engage in trade. But above all the noise and tumult of the crowd could be heard the merchants' voices loudly advertising their products.[3]

Many well-written descriptions not only use sensory information and some sort of spatial description but they also use **movement**. Even in a room with no people in it, an author will make a clock pendulum swing or a curtain wave in the breeze. *Movement* gives interest to the description and helps it come alive.

Now it's your turn. Underline the things in the above paragraph that are moving around Milo. Then circle the things that Milo can see, taste, hear, smell, or touch.

Now it's your turn again. Here is another paragraph from *The Phantom Tollbooth*. Pay close attention to the movement <u>and</u> the direction of the spatial description. Then answer the questions that follow.

> As they [Milo and some friends] ran, tall trees closed in around them and arched gracefully toward the sky. The late-afternoon sunlight leaped lightly from leaf to leaf, slid along branches and down trunks, and dropped finally to the ground in warm, luminous patches. A soft glow filled the air with the kind of light that made everything look sharp and clear and close enough to reach out and touch.[4]

1. What is the direction of the spatial description? _____

2. What is moving? _____

---

[3] Norton Juster, *The Phantom Tollbooth* (New York: Alfred A. Knopf, Inc., 1989), 45.
[4] Ibid., 109.

3. Would you like to be in that place with Milo? Explain. _____

_____

4. **Alliteration** is a series of words beginning with the same sound. Edgar Allan Poe used *alliteration* in his poem "The Bells": "What a <u>t</u>ale of <u>t</u>error, now, their <u>t</u>urbulency <u>t</u>ells!" Where is the alliteration in this paragraph about Milo and the woods?

_____

Skill 13: **Where** are we?

Now it's your turn.   Write one paragraph describing a scene. It may be the fairgrounds, a doctor's office, people gathering for church, teams practicing for a game, diners at a restaurant, friends at a party, etc. Make up the event or use one that you remember.

Make something *move!*

When you have finished writing, reread your work to make sure you have also used specific adjectives and nouns, powerful verbs, a simile or metaphor, a few senses, and a spatial direction. That's a lot to cram into a scene, but you can do it.

Word count: at least 100 words.

A suggested writing schedule:

Day 1   ➡ Describe a scene. Use all of your descriptive skills plus *movement.*

Day 2   ➡ Proofread three times. Make a neat copy.

Remember to use the **Mistake Medic** on page 238 in **YOUR LOCKER**!

Skill 14: **Imitate** me

On page 190 (Skill 12), you read a paragraph about Milo seeking shelter in a patch of woods. It was sunny there, with "warm, luminous patches." There was a "soft glow." These woods sound like a nice place to be.

But what if Milo had just entered a scary or dangerous place? The sunlight wouldn't have "leaped lightly from leaf to leaf." In fact, maybe there wouldn't have been any sunlight at all. In a scary place, the woods might be dark, marshy, and still.

Being careful about the words you use can set the mood for your stories. Your word choice can create a troubling place, an exciting place, a swampy place, or a comforting place. Be aware of the words you use—and use them well.

You have the power to create the scene and the mood.

Now it's your turn. Below is the same three-sentence paragraph about Milo and the woods you read on page 190. The underlined words are the words you will change so that you can create a **dangerous place** for Milo to enter.

As they <u>ran</u>, tall trees <u>closed in</u> around them and <u>arched gracefully</u> toward the sky. The late-afternoon <u>sunlight leaped lightly</u> from leaf to leaf, <u>slid</u> along branches and down trunks, and <u>dropped</u> finally to the ground in <u>warm, luminous patches</u>. A <u>soft glow</u> filled the air with the kind of <u>light</u> that made everything look <u>sharp</u> and <u>clear</u> and <u>close enough to reach out and touch</u>.

D A N G E R O U S   P L A C E

As they _____, tall trees _____ _____ around them and

_____ _____ toward the sky. The late-afternoon

_____ _____ _____ from leaf to leaf,

_____ along branches and down trunks, and _____

finally to the ground in _____ , _____

_____. A _____ _____ filled

the air with the kind of _____ that made everything look _____

and _____ and _____.

Skill 15: Do it **Again**

Now it's your turn.   Create a safe place for Milo, using the paragraph from page 193 (Skill 14) as your pattern. Fill in the blanks below.

As they _____, tall trees _____ _____around them

and _____ _____toward the sky. The late-afternoon

_____ _____ _____from leaf to leaf,

_____ along branches and down trunks, and _____

finally to the ground in _____ , _____

_____. A _____ _____filled

the air with the kind of _____ that made everything look _____

and _____ and _____ .

S
A
F
E

P
L
A
C
E

Here's an example of Milo running to the woods for safety:

As they <u>ran for cover</u>, tall trees <u>hid</u> them and <u>spread leafy umbrellas</u> toward the sky. The late-afternoon <u>downpour plopped loudly</u> from leaf to leaf, <u>gushed over</u> branches and down trunks, and <u>swirled</u> finally to the ground in <u>running, muddy puddles</u>. A <u>thick dampness</u> filled the air with the kind of <u>calm</u> that made everything look <u>misty</u> and <u>still</u> and <u>exciting</u>.

Narration

Skill 1: I can **Imagine** it

Dr. Seuss (Theodor Geisel) had a tough challenge. He had to write a children's book using only 50 different words. He could repeat those words as often as he liked, but he had to stick to those 50 words. Was he successful?

You know the book as *Green Eggs and Ham*.

You have as much imagination as Dr. Seuss did—maybe even more. The name of this chapter is "**Narration**." What is that? *Narration* is telling stories. The stories usually are not true; someone made them up. The writers used their imaginations, and so can you.

Pretend that you have four unrelated objects in front of you: a screwdriver with an orange handle, a fancy blue and silver scarf, a pair of dice, and a red flashlight. You have only 10 minutes to write a story using these items.

Four students working on their own stories and poems came up with these interesting things in honor of Dr. Seuss. Read here and on the next page for the results of their 10-minute imaginations:

> Writing reports and writing stories are two very different skills. If you don't like one, you will probably like the other.

Have you ever met Grandma Clarf,
Who when she was young would sit with her scarf?
When she was young, she could knit with a screwdriver.
Then she learned to be a deep-sea diver.
But now all she does is sit with her dice
And play with her fat, fat, fat, fat mice.

I wanted to find out what was inside the flashlight, so I opened it up with a screwdriver. A genie came out and said, "I am the genie of cheating. If you release me, you may roll these dice. If you roll two sixes, you may have a valuable sash." So I rolled the dice.

"Ah! I got it working," said Mark.

"What?"

"I got the flashlight fixed!"

"Oh!" replied Susan, her scarf slipping off her head. She jerked open the lid of an old box with their one and only screwdriver.

"What's in it, Susan?" Mark whispered.

"I don't know. It's so dark. Can you bring the flashlight?"

"Yes. Ouch! Susan, what was that?"

"It was two dark, small objects, like dice. They came out of that bush over there," she whispered as she pointed.

Instantly, a sudden calm swept over the whole forest.

Notice that not everyone had enough time to fit all four items into their stories. That is because they had to stop writing at the end of the 10 minutes.

When I woke up at five,
I used my flashlight to dive
into my messy room.
Boy, it needs a broom!
There are the dice I lost.
I wonder how much they cost.
So that's where that screwdriver went!
I think I have found my old tent.
Wow! Look at that scarf. Zoom!
Thank goodness, I'm out of my room!

Now it's your turn. Find four unrelated items or ask your teacher to select them for you. Use a separate piece of paper for your creation. Writing this can be even more fun if you write your story while a sibling, friend, or fellow student writes one, too. Then you can exchange stories afterward.

Set the timer. You have only 10 minutes in which to write a story with all four objects in it. Go!

Skill 2: **Reel** me in!

Anything you write should begin with an interesting first sentence or paragraph. In a newspaper article, it is called a lead. In a story, it's called a **hook**.

A *hook* pulls the reader into the story like a flopping fish on the end of a taut line. Here are some guidelines for writing a good hook:

- It should create curiosity about the story.

    - It should have something to do with the story. Deliver what you promise. Don't cheat the reader!

        - After the hook, don't go back and fill in lots of stuff from the past right away. That only stops the story dead in its tracks. Slowly fill in the background information (if you need to) later.

Now it's your turn. Below are some famous hooks you may be familiar with. Write the name of the book below its hook. Then turn the page.

1. There was a boy called Eustace Clarence Scrubb, and he almost deserved it.

2. It was a dull autumn day and Jill Pole was crying behind the gym.

3. Marley was dead: to begin with.

4. All children, except one, grow up.

5. There was once upon a time…
   "A king!" my little readers will instantly exclaim.
   No, children, you are wrong. There was once upon a time a piece of wood.

6. "Where's Papa going with that ax?" said Fern to her mother as they were setting the table for breakfast.

Now it's your turn again. Below are some hooks written by fifth- through eighth-graders. They did not have to finish the stories; they only had to write the hooks. Circle the ones that interest you. You will not be required to finish them, but you may want to later, just for fun.

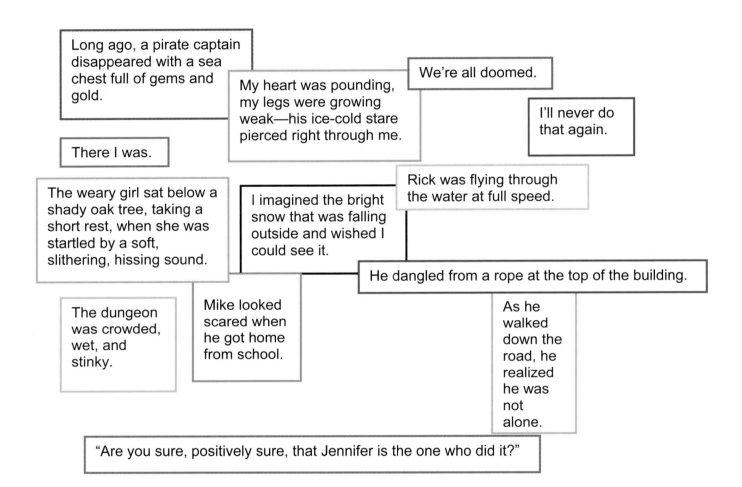

Long ago, a pirate captain disappeared with a sea chest full of gems and gold.

We're all doomed.

My heart was pounding, my legs were growing weak—his ice-cold stare pierced right through me.

I'll never do that again.

There I was.

The weary girl sat below a shady oak tree, taking a short rest, when she was startled by a soft, slithering, hissing sound.

I imagined the bright snow that was falling outside and wished I could see it.

Rick was flying through the water at full speed.

He dangled from a rope at the top of the building.

The dungeon was crowded, wet, and stinky.

Mike looked scared when he got home from school.

As he walked down the road, he realized he was not alone.

"Are you sure, positively sure, that Jennifer is the one who did it?"

Skill 3: Here, Fishy, **Fishy!**

Now that you've read some famous and not-so-famous hooks, it's time to create some of your own.

Now it's your turn.

1. Write three hooks.
2. Find a friend, sibling, or classmate who will also write three hooks.
3. Exchange the hooks with each other and write a story from one of them for 10 minutes.
4. Don't start the timer until you begin writing.

A suggested writing schedule:

Days 1-2   ☐ Write the hooks. Find the friends, exchange the hooks, and write the story from a hook. Write for 10 minutes. No need to proofread. Have fun!

Skill 4: Change my World

How would Robin Hood react if you plunked him down in the middle of a modern city? What would his problems be? How would he find food? What would people say about his cute green tights?

What would Mary Poppins do if you snatched her away from the Banks' house and moved her into yours? Would she set everything straight—including your bedroom?

Imagine taking Caractacus Pott from his *Chitty Chitty Bang Bang: A Magical Car* setting and putting him and his family in a wild jungle in the Amazon River Basin. What would he do? How would they eat? How would he, with all his inventing skills, get them back home?

> Moving an established character from his old setting to a new one is a fun way to play with both the character and a setting.

Below is the <u>beginning</u> of a story written by a boy in the seventh grade. He took a familiar character—Ebenezer Scrooge from *A Christmas Carol* by Charles Dickens—and made him a worker in a charity organization. Read to see what happens as Scrooge finds himself in a strange place:

> Scrooge had said over and over again that anybody who worked for a charity organization was a pigheaded fool, but this is a story of how he found himself in that very position.
>
> It all began one fine spring day when children were playing, birds were singing, the sun was shining, and Scrooge was inside his dark, dank house counting his money. Suddenly he was somewhere else.
>
> Scrooge was in a yard in his nightgown! A young lady in black and white clothing approached him and said, "Shame on you, sir! Drunken in the middle of the lawn."
>
> "I am not drunk. Too expensive."
>
> "Oh," she exclaimed, "are you looking for a job?"
>
> Scrooge, still dazed, muttered, "Yes, yes. I suppose so."
>
> The nun, for it was she in the black and white clothing, said, "Good. You may work in the kitchen."
>
> An hour later, when Scrooge was beginning to recover his wits and had gotten some clothing, he plucked up the courage to ask a young man where he was.
>
> The young man answered with some surprise, "Why, at St. Mary's Rescue Mission for Children."
>
> Scrooge blanched and, at the last two words, nearly fainted dead away. After that, he demanded to see someone in charge.

As you probably can guess, his experiences go from bad to worse until he is transported back to his own house. This student ended his story by stating that this strange visit to St. Mary's softened Scrooge's heart just enough to get him ready to change later that winter when the three spirits eventually visited him.

You can be creative too. Read these writing ideas to get your imagination pumping:

- Pooh, Piglet, Eeyore, and Christopher Robin in Middle Earth surrounded by orcs
- Legolas and the Black Riders in Sherwood Forest with Robin Hood
- Anne Shirley Blythe and her children in a Roman amphitheater
- A Narnian dwarf at a children's summer camp
- Qui-Gon Jinn in Hollywood
- Garfield (the cat) in Snoopy's comic strip (*Peanuts*®)
- Jonah in modern America
- Luke Skywalker in your town

Now it's your turn. Write a short story in which you move a fictional character into a new setting (time and place). The new setting can be from another book, a modern or historical place, or one you make up. The fictional character has to keep his original personality.

Describe the new setting so the reader will know it as well as your character does. When your character experiences something, so should your reader. Use the descriptive skills you learned in the last chapter.

Pause to think about the problems your character will face in this new time and place. How will he or she cope? Get food? Find friends? Deal with the different culture? How will your character get to the new place and get back home? Word count: at least 300 words.

A suggested writing schedule:

Days 1-3   ⇨ Put an existing fictional character into a different setting and write a short story about what happens.

Day 4   ⇨ Proofread three times. Make a neat copy.

Remember to use the **Mistake Medic** on page 238 in **YOUR LOCKER!**

Skill 5: What a **Character!**

Some writers work hard to construct a character. They write pages of background information about the person, completely making him up—his likes, family, habits, appearance, ethnic and educational background, etc. Only after the character is completely built will the writer put him into the story.

> The more you write, the more you will find the method that works best for you.

Other writers have a partial idea of what their character will be like. Then they put the character into the story and see what he does and how he reacts to other characters and situations.

Which way is the best way to create a character? Believe it or not, both methods can be successful.

In this workbook, you will practice the first method—constructing a character.

Now it's your turn. Create a new character. Fill in the information about him or her by using the headings below. Use separate pieces of paper.

1. Gender, age, appearance, name
2. Where he or she lives and in what time period
3. Ethnic background (race, color, country, culture, etc.)
4. Personality (shy, pushy, friendly, organized, scatterbrained, etc.)
5. Family members
6. Education
7. Likes and dislikes
8. Habits
9. Religious background and beliefs
10. Hobbies
11. What he or she dreams of doing someday
12. What he or she fears
13. Friends
14. Hardest and easiest things for him or her to do
15. Favorite books, movies, and songs
16. Pets
17. Anything else you can think of

A suggested writing schedule:

Days 1-2   ☐ Create a new character. Use the list above as you ponder your character's history and personality. No need to proofread.

Skill 6: **Howdy**, Stranger

You have created a new character. You have also given him or her a personality and a history. By now you should know your character fairly well. But nobody else does. It is time to introduce your character to the world!

Now it's your turn.   Write a paragraph describing your character's favorite place. Use your descriptive skills. Where is your character in this place? What will he or she be doing? Where will he or she sit? Any music? Friends around?
  Word count: at least 100 words.

A suggested writing schedule:

Days 1-2   ➤ Write about your character's favorite place and put him or her in it. The reader wants to see what your character will do there!

Day 3   ➤ Proofread three times. Make a neat copy.

Remember to use the **Mistake Medic** on page 238 in **YOUR LOCKER**!

Skill 7: Your character's **Character**

Now that you've put your character in his favorite place, it's time to show your reader what kind of person you've created. What is his defining characteristic (his major trait)? Is he greedy? Generous? Friendly? A liar? In other words, what is a major trait of your character?

Now it's your turn. Your character is in his or her favorite place when, suddenly, someone walks in. Who walks in and what happens next? That's up to you. Use this new person and the things that happen next to show the reader your character's trait—good or bad.

If your character is greedy, you won't ever say that he's greedy. You will create a situation to show how he acts in a greedy way. Then your reader will understand that your character is greedy.

Is your character friendly? Then create a situation to show that, no matter what, he will try to be a friendly person. You will never mention the word *friendly*, but by the end of the situation, your reader will pick up on the fact that your character is definitely friendly.

Word count: at least 250 words.

A suggested writing schedule:

Days 1–3   ⮕ Write the situation to show your character's trait.

Day 4   ⮕ Proofread three times. Make a neat copy.

Remember to use the **Mistake Medic** on page 238 in **YOUR LOCKER**!

Skill 8: It's all in your **Point of View**

Every story is written from someone's point of view (POV). You don't simply read a book; you experience the story through someone's eyes, or you look over someone's shoulder. In *Peter Pan*, for example, you look over Wendy's, Peter's, and sometimes even Hook's shoulders, as told by a narrator.

Today's writers often use one of these two points of view: **first person** and **third-person limited**.

Read the boxes below in order to identify which POV you are reading. Check your book's narration—the part that isn't dialogue—to know which point of view the author is using. Then check the key words listed below and turn the page.

First Person

You see the story through one person's eyes, and that person is telling you the story ("I was happy").

You know what that person is thinking or feeling, and he is usually the protagonist. Sometimes a minor character tells the story in first person, as Luke writes the book of Acts ("We boarded...," "We put out to sea...," etc.).

Treasure Island and *The Time Machine* are examples of first-person point of view.

Third-Person Limited

You see the story over one, two, or three people's shoulders, told by an invisible narrator ("He was happy").

Limited means you limit the POV to one, two, or three people—not everyone. You know what a select few are thinking and feeling.

Charlotte's Web, Peter Pan, and the book of *Esther* are examples of third-person limited point of view.

The Key to Identifying POV

The following words occur in the <u>narrative</u> portion of a story written in first person, **rarely** in the <u>narrative</u> of a third-person limited POV:

I, me, my, mine, myself
we, us, our, ours, ourselves

Exception: The only time any of those pronouns listed in the key occur in a third-person POV is when the author or narrator intrudes himself into the story.

Mr. Collodi does this in *Pinocchio*. Turn to page 197 (Skill 2) and read #5. Collodi speaks to the readers as though they were in front of him, something writers in other generations used to do. However, Pinocchio's story is told in third person by a usually invisible narrator: "The puppet returned to the town" and "Only think of poor Pinocchio's terror at the sight of the monster."

Sir James Barrie also intrudes himself into the text of *Peter Pan:* "In they went; I don't know how there was room for them, but you can squeeze very tight in the Neverland." Even though "I" is occasionally in the narrative, *Peter Pan* is still in third-person POV, a narrator telling us about Wendy, Peter, and Hook.

So, other than a writer intruding himself into a story, the pronouns on page 205 only occur in a first-person narrative. Really.

Now it's your turn. Read the following 10 excerpts and determine their point of view. If the point of view is first person, put a "1" in the blank. If the point of view is third-person limited, put a "3" in the blank. <u>Underline</u> key words if the selection is in first person. No authors are intruding in these examples; there are no tricks.

_____1. His children, too, were as ragged and wild as if they belonged to nobody. His son Rip, an urchin begotten in his own likeness, promised to inherit the habits, with the old clothes, of his father. (*Rip Van Winkle* by Washington Irving)

_____2. For my part, I cannot say that my reflections were very agreeable. I knew that we were on an island, for Jack had said so, but whether it was inhabited or not I did not know. (*The Coral Island* by R. M. Ballantyne)

_____3. After darkly looking at his leg and at me several times, he came closer to my tombstone, took me by both arms, and tilted me back as far as he could hold me; so that his eyes looked most powerfully down into mine, and mine looked most helplessly up into his. (*Great Expectations* by Charles Dickens)

_____4. A few minutes later the little Prince of Wales was garlanded with Tom's fluttering odds and ends, and the little Prince of Pauperdom was tricked out in the gaudy plumage of royalty. (*The Prince and the Pauper* by Mark Twain)

_____5. She had been lying awake turning from side to side for about an hour, when suddenly something made her sit up in bed and turn her head toward the door listening. She listened and she listened. (*The Secret Garden* by Frances Hodgson Burnett)

_____6. His sobs woke Wendy, and she sat up in bed. She was not alarmed to see a stranger crying on the nursery floor; she was only pleasantly interested. (*Peter Pan* by Sir James Barrie)

_____7. You may fancy the terror I was in! I should have leaped out and run for it, if I had found the strength; but my limbs and heart alike misgave me. (*Treasure Island* by Robert Louis Stevenson)

_____8. But the next event to be related is terrible indeed. Its very memory, even now, makes my soul shudder and my blood run cold. (*Journey to the Center of the Earth* by Jules Verne)

_____9. The noise at night would have been annoying to me ordinarily, but I didn't mind it in the present circumstances, because it kept me from hearing the quacks detaching legs and arms from the day's cripples. (*A Connecticut Yankee in King Arthur's Court* by Mark Twain)

_____10. Two of the strongest monkeys caught Mowgli under the arms and swung off with him through the tree-tops, twenty feet at a bound. (*The Jungle Book* by Rudyard Kipling)

Skill 9: I had the **Strangest Dream!**

The story of Daniel in the lions' den is, amazingly, *not* told from Daniel's point of view. We know nothing of how he is feeling as he is lowered into the dangerous den. But we do know exactly how the king is feeling! The narrator of this true story chose to tell the story from the king's perspective, in third-person POV ("The king did this" and "The king was troubled").

> The King was troubled and impatient, and he couldn't sleep. How was Daniel feeling?

The invisible narrator in the David and Goliath story looks over David's shoulder. We know what David is thinking and feeling. We know why he attacks a champion many times his size. The story is in third person ("David did this" and "David was angry") because we learn about David from the invisible narrator, not from David himself.

Find Jonah in the Bible. Is it in first person ("I went to Nineveh") or third-person limited ("He went to Nineveh")? Write the answer here:

_____.

Read Daniel 2 in your Bible. Nebuchadnezzar had a dream, and it is told in third-person limited. You see over only two characters' shoulders: Nebuchadnezzar's and Daniel's. When you read about the king, you know what he is thinking, feeling, and doing. When you read about Daniel, you know what *he* is thinking, feeling, and doing. There are other people in this story, but you never see over their shoulders. You never know what they are thinking or feeling.

Below and on the next page you will find an example of this story written from someone else's point of view. A boy in the eighth grade invented a clothes dresser for the king. The whole episode is from the clothes dresser's point of view as he tells his story—in first person—in a letter of 259 words.

Dear Naomi,
    I, Joshua Benjamin, Nebuchadnezzar's clothes dresser, was rudely awakened by a shrill scream in the middle of the night. Fifteen minutes later, someone was pounding on my door. It was the king's bodyguard.
    He said, "The king needs his robes immediately."
    I rose, quite mystified as to what was going on, and quickly rushed to the royal

closet. Then I grabbed a purple velvet robe and ran in a panic to the king's room. I quickly tried to dress him, but in my haste I ripped the robe. He ran out anyway, but I'm afraid there will be serious repercussions.

I, being naturally curious, followed. He assembled all his prophets and magicians (who are grossly overrated, trust me!) and asked them to interpret a bizarre dream. None of them even took a guess.

Oh, hurray! I had found a way to get back in the king's favor. My friend Daniel was a whiz at this dream stuff.

I went forward and bowed low, trying to hide my pent-up excitement. I respectfully told him about Daniel. The king immediately sent for him. Daniel came and interpreted the dream. Boy, was it a bad one!

My reward for finding a prophet who could interpret the dream and for ripping the robe was, instead of my life being taken, being sold into slavery! I hope this letter reaches you. Pray for me. I won't be able to bid you farewell.

Your loving husband,
Joshua

P. S. – Give the kids my love.
P. P. S. – I am being sold to Persia.

Now it's your turn. Write this true story of Nebuchadnezzar's dream. If you tell it in first person, you may use someone already in the story, or you may make someone up. If you tell it in third-person limited, choose an imaginary or real person whose shoulder the invisible narrator—you—will be looking over. Word count: at least 250 words.

(Note: If you don't want to rewrite a Bible story, choose a fairy tale and rewrite it from someone else's point of view. For instance, you may remember that Disney's *Cinderella* is not always from Cinderella's point of view but from the point of view of the mice who are helping her.)

A suggested writing schedule:

Days 1-3   ☐ Read Daniel 2. Choose an existing person from the chapter or make up a character. Choose the point of view. Write the story.

Day 4   ☐ Proofread three times. Make a neat copy.

Remember to use the **Mistake Medic** on page 238 in **YOUR LOCKER!**

Skill 10: But **Why?**

When a character makes a choice or a decision, she has to have a good reason why she makes it. She has to have a **motivation.** The author cannot let her characters do things without letting you know why they do them or why they make certain choices.

When Wendy Darling goes to Neverland with Peter Pan, she has to have a *motivation* for going. After all, she is leaving her pleasant home and putting her brothers in jeopardy (Indians, Captain Hook, a crocodile, etc.). Why does she do it?

Sir James Barrie puts the motivation (the reasons) in. He makes sure the reader knows that Wendy is an adventuress and that she loves the tales of Peter Pan. The reader sees that Wendy is brave when she deals with Peter's shadow. And the reader learns that the lost boys have no mother, something Wendy is very good at being. She sees the need and the adventure—and she's off!

What is Captain Hook's motivation for hating Peter Pan?

In any story in which children or teens are the main characters, a writer has to include a believable reason why they don't go to the adults in the story for help. Obviously, if they go to the adults, the story most likely would be over. So the writer has to think of a way around that.

Unfortunately, in many modern stories, adults are portrayed as stupid or mean, and that is why the children or teens don't go to them for help with their problem. A Christian writer of any age, however, will respect adults as well as children. So there have to be other, workable reasons for the children or teen characters not to go to the adults.

Now it's your turn. Write **three separate reasons** why the children or teens might not ask the adults for help when faced with a problem. Let your motivations be respectful of the adults in the story. You may refer to stories for ideas.

1.

2.

3.

Skill 11: I've got this **Problem...**

When the main character's problem is big enough and interesting enough, it can draw the reader into the character's difficulties. The reader will want to keep reading. But if the main character's problem is a paper cut, who cares? So what?

Let's make it worse: The main character, a likeable guy named Pete, has a paper cut, and it gets badly infected, and he's in a remote area of the world where there are no doctors, and he has to have his whole hand amputated if he doesn't get help soon, and the boat carrying his medicine has to be quarantined because of an outbreak of typhoid fever—ah, then we care!

> The size of the conflict can determine the size of the hero— if the hero doesn't cheat.

In many movies and books today, a minor theme seems to be this: "Sometimes, you gotta break a few rules!" But for writers who love the Lord, this way of **resolving the conflict** (fixing the problem) is not a permanent option.

A character who breaks the rules throughout most of the story must finally realize that this is getting him nowhere. This way you can show the negative consequences of breaking rules or show your character wising up and doing it the right way by the end of the story. But *resolving the conflict* by breaking the rules doesn't do anybody any good.

On the other hand, *you don't want a quick fix for the problem.* The reader feels cheated, and the conflict feels silly. Don't be afraid to let things go from bad to worse. Keep the conflict going and let the main character make bad choices or get into more trouble until he has to make a major decision. That's the crisis to which the whole story has been building, so it had better be worth the struggle!

> Don't fix the problem too fast. Let your character squirm.

Now it's your turn. On the next page is a scenario (a situation). It is your job to write Friend A out of the problem and to resolve the conflict. Let it go from bad to worse—no quick fixes. Then let your character somehow resolve the problem in a way that will honor God.

You choose the genders of the best friends, their names, and their ages. You also choose the point of view from which to tell this story.

Word count: at least 300 words.

Scenario

Two best friends work together at Gershwin's U-Pick Farm for the summer. They have been best friends all their lives. At the farm, they pick some of the fruit and vegetables for the customers, restock shelves, and work behind the counter as cashiers.

Today, Mrs. Gershwin (the boss) comes in and realizes that there is money missing from the cash register. She has been suspicious for a week, but now she knows for sure. She accuses both of the friends.

By the end of the day, Best Friend A realizes that it is Best Friend B who has been stealing the money for CDs and computer games.

How does Best Friend A find out? What does Best Friend A do? How does Best Friend B react when he or she realizes that Best Friend A knows? Can the friends remain friends? Do they keep their jobs? What happens?

A suggested writing schedule:

Days 1-3   ⇨ Write the story. Resolve the conflict.

Day 4   ⇨ Proofread three times. Make a neat copy.

Remember to use the **Mistake Medic** on page 238 in **YOUR LOCKER!**

Skill 12: Talk, talk, **Talk!**

Some older stories have very little conversation in them, but today's writers often like to use a lot of conversation in their stories. And readers like to read it. Writers know that **dialogue** (written conversation) does something important in a story:

- It moves the plot/action along.
  - It shows what the characters are like.
    - It breaks up paragraphs of narration and description.

The *dialogue* you write should sound like what your characters would say. Would a modern person say, "Whatsoever thou desirest, my love apple, is that task which I exist to perform"? Would a person from 500 years ago say, "Yeah, whatever"? I think not.

On this page and the next is an example of dialogue interwoven with narration. In this story, a Narnian dwarf is transported to Northern England a few hundred years ago. At this point in the story, the dwarf has just appeared in England and finds himself hidden behind some curtains. Observe how the dialogue tells you what the plot is (what is happening) and shows the reader what the characters are like. A girl in the eighth grade wrote this, but the following is only the <u>beginning</u> of her story.

Dialogue interwoven with narration is called *dovetailing.*

Rubbing my eyes, I am sitting 'neath a windowsill in the parlor of a farmhouse. Hid by a little bit of curtains hanging o'er my round, bearded, handsome face, I am quite bewildered, and so ye would be also if ye had blacked out in your comfy little cottage and appeared someplace strange.

As loud knocking commenced at the large, heavy oaken door, I heard the residents of the home stirring by the parlor fireside.

"Peter, the door!" cried a startled man. I heard the man rise out of a rocking chair and stride to the other side of the fire so he could be in view of the door.

I moved the heavy curtains enough to know I wasn't in Narnia at all. Before I could inquire my whereabouts, however, Peter gave an exclamation at the door.

From the fireside, Peter's father, or so I guessed, asked the newcomer, "Why are ye here, brother Duncan, at so late a time, and who are those men 'round the horses?"

"Why I be here is to be answered at once if ye let me in."

I perceived water pouring down his clean-cut face and wool plaid clothing as he appeared in the light of the fire. Peter let his uncle in.

"Brother, I am come to request Peter and ye to join us Highlanders who believe that something worthwhile must be accomplished—to fight the British for Scotland's freedom. Our leader is Prince Charlie. He sent those of us who have kinsmen down this way to urge ye to join us in this war for freedom. So, what think ye, my brother?"

Following a thick silence in which I could tell Peter's father was praying silently, he spoke to his wife.

"What say ye, Eliza?"

"Have ye any leaning from the Lord? If so, ye may go."

"I do have a leaning from God to go."

"My consent is given, then. Shall we prepare?" she replied quietly, blinking back tears.

As they began preparations to leave, I decided to make myself a wee bit more noticed, so I inched toward the fire, which was opposite my window. All of a sudden, to my great annoyance, a horrid, shrill, panicking scream tore through the room at a tremendous rate.

Now, who might that have been, ye may ask. 'Twas a lass no taller than I, and she was sitting by the hearth with a cup of whey in her hands. Evidently, she was the first one to discover me.

Now, if ye think I'm as ugly as she made me out to be, don't ye squawk like she did!

"Why, Miss Adelheid! Ye know ye aren't to scream so, much less at a visitor," her father reminded her.

"Father, kill that thing!" she whispered hoarsely, pointing to me.

Now it's your turn. Answer the questions below.

1. What did the dialogue tell you about the plot?

2. What did the dialogue tell you about the characters?

3. What point of view is it written in?   ☐ first person
                                               ☐ third-person limited

4. From whose POV is it written?

5. Underline the dialogue (spoken words) and notice the good balance this student has between dialogue and narration.

Skill 13: Their **lips** are moving, but...

Now it's your turn. Get a movie on video or on DVD. Turn off the sound. Now write a new dialogue for the characters in one scene. The silly example below shows you how to set up the names of the characters and their words:

Frank is tied in a chair, back to back with his friend Henry. They are alone in the room.

FRANK

Knock, knock.

HENRY

I've got better things to do than play stupid games with you. Help me get this rope loose.

FRANK

Egypt.

HENRY

Can you reach that knife in your boot?

FRANK

'E gypped me when he took my knife and tied me up.

HENRY

Isn't there someone else around here I can be tied to?

A suggested writing schedule:

Days 1-3   ➡ Write at least three pages of new dialogue for a movie scene.

Day 4   ➡ Proofread three times. Make a neat copy.

Remember to use the **Mistake Medic** on page 238 in **YOUR LOCKER**!

Skill 14: A **Cramped** conversation

People don't always speak in complete sentences.   Pay attention to the conversations you are in, and you will notice this right away.   Be aware of this when you write your dialogue.

Below are examples of how to punctuate dialogue.   Note carefully the commas, quotation marks, capitalization, etc.   Notice, also, that the commas and end marks go on the *inside* of the end quotation marks.   Quotation marks, commas, and end marks appear in colors to emphasize them.

STATEMENTS:

"I just found my swimming medal in the dryer," said Amy.

Amy said, "I just found my swimming medal in the dryer."

"I just found my swimming medal," said Amy, "in the dryer."

"I just found my swimming medal," Amy said. "It was in the dryer."

QUESTIONS:

Roberto asked, "Have you been to the circus since they added the lions?"

"Have you been to the circus since they added the lions?" asked Roberto.

"Have you been to the circus," asked Roberto, "since they added the lions?"

"Have you been to the circus?" asked Roberto.   "They just added the lions!"

You can also find help in your grammar book.

Each speaker starts a new paragraph. Read below to see how this works. The example contains 129 words.

"Have you been to the circus?" asked Roberto. "They just added the lions!" He remembered the deafening roar he had heard last night as one of the lions challenged the trainer. Just the thought of that roar made Roberto's blood tingle.

"No," said Juan, "but I don't want to miss the jugglers."

"The jugglers! They are nothing!"

"Then you haven't seen them juggling their torches!" Juan stood on the pavement and imitated a juggler moving through his routine. Then he pretended to miss a torch, and he watched as they all fell through the air and hit the pavement, one invisible torch at a time. Juan and Roberto both laughed.

"What happens when they catch a torch by the wrong end?" Roberto asked.

"You'll have to see for yourself!"

As the conversation moves along, there is no need for a *he said* with each quotation. Once you have established who is speaking, the reader can follow who comes next.

Now it's your turn. Write a conversation between two people who are stuck on an elevator. They are opposite genders from each other. You choose the age and their occupation or grade. Show the reader how different these two people are from one another and how they react to their situation. Include their actions, as the example above does.

Word count: at least 200 words.

A suggested writing schedule:

Days 1-2   ☐ Write the dialogue and some action.

Day 3   ☐ Check the dialogue punctuation and paragraphs.

Day 4   ☐ Proofread three times. Make a neat copy.

Remember to use the **Mistake Medic** on page 238 in **YOUR LOCKER!**

Skill 15: And the **Moral** of the story is...

You are probably familiar with Aesop's fables—short stories with a moral. At the end of the story about the dog in a manger, the moral states that it is mean to keep others from getting what you don't even use. At the end of "Androcles and the Lion," you find that noble souls don't ever forget a kindness.

Those fables exist to prove the moral. And they do it in very clever ways, often using animals. For inspiration, go to the library and read a few of Aesop's fables or fables from other lands.

Now it's your turn. Below is a fable written by a boy in the sixth grade. He used 200 words. Read it and write a moral for the end of the story.

The Sly Fox and the Three Chickens

Once upon a time a chicken named Rosie lived on a farm with her two sisters, Rachel and Renée. One day a sly fox came to the barnyard and asked them to a picnic. When they arrived at the picnic area, they threw a Frisbee to each other. Having a very strong arm, the sly fox purposely threw the Frisbee as far as he could and told the chickens to go and find it. While they were gone, the sly fox quickly dug a hole in the ground and covered it with leaves so as to disguise it from the chickens.

When Rosie, Rachel, and Renée returned with the Frisbee, the sly fox again threw the Frisbee into the woods. For a second time, the three chickens went to look for the Frisbee. And again the sly fox dug another hole and covered it with leaves. Finally, the sly fox threw the Frisbee one last time into the woods. While the three chickens went to find it, the sly fox completed his last trap.

When Rosie, Rachel, and Renée returned with the Frisbee, they each fell into the sly fox's traps. And the fox ate them all up for lunch.

MORAL:

Skill 16: You can **Lead A Horse** to water...

Now it's your turn. Choose an interesting moral, saying, or proverb. It can be silly or serious. Then write a fable to prove the moral, saying, or proverb. Include your interesting saying at the *end* of your fable. Below are some examples of morals. You can use one of these, choose one of your own, or make one up.

Word count: at least 200 words.

SAYINGS

1. Haste makes waste.
2. The wise woman builds her house, but with her own hands the foolish one tears hers down (Proverbs 14:1).
3. A stitch in time saves nine.
4. He who walks with the wise grows wise, but a companion of fools suffers harm (Proverbs 13:20).
5. Absence makes the heart grow fonder.
6. Blessed are the merciful, for they will be shown mercy (Matthew 5:7).
7. People who live in glass houses shouldn't throw stones.
8. It is better to find a whole worm in an apple than half a worm.
9. Idle hands are the devil's tools.
10. Be part of the solution, not the problem.

A suggested writing schedule:

Day 1   ❑ Choose or invent a moral, saying, or proverb.

Days 2-3   ❑ Write the fable to prove the moral. Use animals if appropriate. Include the moral at the end of your fable.

Day 4   ❑ Proofread three times. Make a neat copy.

Remember to use the **Mistake Medic** on page 238 in **YOUR LOCKER!**

Skill 17: They're **Everywhere!**

It is amazing but true that there are patterns of three everywhere. Even in the Bible, they are all over the place: three persons in the Trinity, Jonah three days in the belly of the great fish, three children of Noah, three choices David had to make after he had sinned by taking a census, and Jesus three days in the grave. No doubt you can find more.

Our Western culture likes the rhythm of three. Three strikes and you're out. Three beats to a measure in waltzes. Third time's a charm.

Think of all the stories that have threes in them. "Goldilocks and the Three Bears" is filled with threes. "The Three Little Pigs" also has many patterns of three, even in what the pig says: "Not by the hair of my chinny, chin, chin!" And how many wishes does a magic fish usually grant?

Now it's your turn. Turn back to page 218 (Skill 15) and count the patterns of three in the short fable. List them here:

Think of other patterns of three in stories, in the Bible, or in life. Write down at least five examples.

1.

2.

3.

4.

5.

Skill 18: Open, **Sesame!**

You are familiar with many types of short stories. When you were younger, someone probably read them to you. Read the list below and see how many stories you recognize. <u>Underline</u> the stories you have read or heard:

Fairy Tales: "Cinderella," "Sleeping Beauty," "Snow White," "The Little Mermaid," "Little Red Riding Hood," "Hansel and Gretel," "The Tinder Box," "The Elves and the Shoemaker"

Tall Tales: Paul Bunyan, Pecos Bill, and Slue-foot Sue stories

Just So Stories (by Rudyard Kipling): "How the Camel Got His Hump," "How the Leopard Got His Spots," and "How the Alphabet Was Made" are only a few stories in this engaging book. There are others stories of this kind that Kipling didn't write. One is about how the sea became salty.

Parables: "The Sower and the Seed," "The Lost Sheep," "The Prodigal Son"

You are blessed with a rich heritage of stories from many cultures. To stir your imagination, go to the library and read some books containing these stories and more.

Below and on the next page is the *beginning* of a fairy tale written by a boy in the eighth grade. <u>Underline</u> his pattern of three.

Forbidden Emerald

As the fog lifted, it revealed the glistening crystals of frost. When the sun broke through the clouds, it turned the forest into a shimmering throne room reflecting God's glory.

"Blessed be the Lord God who made heaven and earth," praised the king.

After viewing this sight, the king returned his thoughts to his hunting. Scanning the forest, his attention was captured by a thicket that was thrashing wildly. The object of the commotion turned out to be an enormous buck that had its antlers stuck in the thicket. As the king drew his bow, a voice called out.

"Do not kill me, and you shall see that with a kind deed I shall repay thee."

The king started and looked around. Seeing no one, he began to draw his bow again, and again the mysterious voice called out.

"This deed shall come at a time of need."

"Show yourself, you who speaks in rhyme," the king called out.

"It is I, the deer, who is to you so near."

Astonished, the king slid off the back of his horse and released the deer's antlers from the thicket. Once free, the deer bounded away without another word.

"I must be out of my mind. A talking deer, and I let dinner get away, too."

The king continued on, determined not to let the next creature escape.

When he came to a clearing, he sent his falcon to see if it could get a rabbit or two. As he had hoped, the bird swooped down into the grass. Upon its return, he saw that the falcon had a small rabbit. When the bird put the rabbit into the king's hand, the king saw that the rabbit was not dead, as he had expected. As the king reached for his knife to slay the rabbit, another mysterious voice called out.

"Kill me not, King Ceilingot, and something for you I will do."

"Could it be this rabbit who said this?" exclaimed the king. "First a deer and now a rabbit."

He set down the rabbit and watched it hop away.

"What a day this has been," thought the king. All of a sudden he heard a voice screech.

"Dear King, help me lest I perish! Save me if my life thou dost cherish!"

Turning around, the king spied a wolf preying on a little squirrel. Quickly, the king raised his bow and let loose the arrow. It flew straight and pierced the heart of the wolf. The king, after recovering from his surprise, asked, "How is it that all of you animals can talk?"

"My dear King, it is because of the jewel of old. Alas, the queen has touched the forbidden emerald," rhymed the squirrel as he scurried away.

Now it's your turn. Write a fairy tale, tall tale, *Just So* story, or parable. Glean ideas from the rich heritage of stories at your library. Use your imagination, and use a pattern of three.

As you write your story, you have a few choices to make. Ask yourself, "Whose story is this?" The above story is the king's story told from a narrator's POV. But it would be very different if the queen told her story.

After you have decided who the main character will be, you have another decision. You have to decide which point of view you are going to use—first person or third-person limited. In other words, is your main character going to tell the story, or is a narrator going to tell the story as he looks over the main character's shoulder? Word count: at least 300 words.

A suggested writing schedule:

Day 1   ➡ Read some fairy tales, etc., to get ideas.

Days 2-4   ➡ Write a fairy tale, etc. Use a pattern of three.

Day 5   ➡ Proofread three times. Make a neat copy.

Remember to use the **Mistake Medic** on page 238 in **YOUR LOCKER!**

Skill 19: It was a dark and **Stormy** night...

Many students cannot get enough of writing stories. Some of them keep a notebook handy in order to remember their interesting ideas and use them later. They daydream, mulling over characters and plots. They even write stories when no one assigns them any.

Are these students crazy? They're writing when no one tells them to!

No, they aren't crazy—they're creative.

If this describes you, then the following list will spark your imagination. In fact, you will probably be able to add many more ideas for stories at the end of the list.

If this doesn't describe you, the list will be quite helpful to you the next time your teacher says, "Write a story." It will give you ideas that you don't have to come up with yourself. So put fresh batteries in your imagination and read on.

Write a Story...

- that begins like this: If I had known what kind of day it was going to be, I never would have gotten out of bed.
- about a pet who gets into trouble.
- about a lonely person and how he or she gets un-lonely.
- that begins with an argument.
- about a person who owns a collection of something (rocks, stamps, stuffed animals, insects, etc.). For one day, your character is the same size as the objects in his collection. How did he get small?   What troubles will come his way? How will he return to normal size?
- about a person caught in a storm. You choose the type of storm, how your character got there, and how he survives.
- about a person going back in time, trying to change something awful that happened.
- using an animal that can talk, like Bambi, or Charlotte and Wilbur in *Charlotte's Web*.
- that includes an interesting historical figure.
- of Jack and his beanstalk from the giant's point of view.
- about a toy that comes to life.
- about a pacifist (someone who doesn't believe in fighting). But his friend is attacked, and your character has to defend him. How will he do it?
- about a person who loses an ability (can't see, speak, walk, taste, etc.).
- about a person who discovers that he or she has a superpower.
- about a character who is an inanimate object (a chair, a car, a bike, a shoe, and so forth).

- about meeting your hero.
- using as many of this week's spelling or vocabulary words as you can.
- that is a fairy tale in which someone is granted three wishes.
- about a family during a holiday or vacation.
- about a girl (if you are a boy) or about a boy (if you are a girl).
- about what would happen if a fictional character (Captain Hook, Aslan, the Cowardly Lion, etc.) came to your home or class.

Now it's your turn. Don't stop now. You probably have some ideas you'd like to add to the list. Keep the above list and your additions handy for the next time a story assignment looms ahead or the urge to write a story hits you.

YOUR STORY IDEAS:

Optional **Now it's your turn:** Choose one of the stories and write it!

Remember to use the **Mistake Medic** on page 238 in **YOUR LOCKER**!

Poetry

Skill 1: Haiku

Haiku (hi' coo) is a poem form that comes from Japan, is usually about nature, and can be spoken in one breath. It does not rhyme. **Syllables** are important in a haiku. The first line has five, the second line has seven, and the third line has five again. Count them in the poems below. Can you say them in one breath?

> The trees, tall and round,
> branches swaying in the wind.
> Will they fly away?
> (by a seventh-grade boy)

> Oh, little sparrow,
> singing deeply from within,
> how you please thy God.
> (by an eighth-grade girl)

> The sun, a hot ball,
> sinks into the cold ocean.
> I look for the steam.

Now it's your turn. Write a haiku.

5 _____

7 _____

5 _____

Skill 2: A Cinquain

A cinquain (sin' cane, alternate is sing' kwane) is a poem of five lines and is often about something in nature. It does not rhyme. Some forms of cinquains count syllables; this form counts words. The number of words for each line is 1, 2, 3, 4, 1. Below is the pattern for the parts of speech. There are no periods at the ends of the lines and very little capitalization. Examples are in the boxes:

Line 1   title   (1 noun)
Line 2   description of title   (2 adjectives)
Line 3   action of title   (3 verbs)
Line 4   statement of feeling or mood   (4-word phrase)
Line 5   repeated title or synonym   (1 noun)

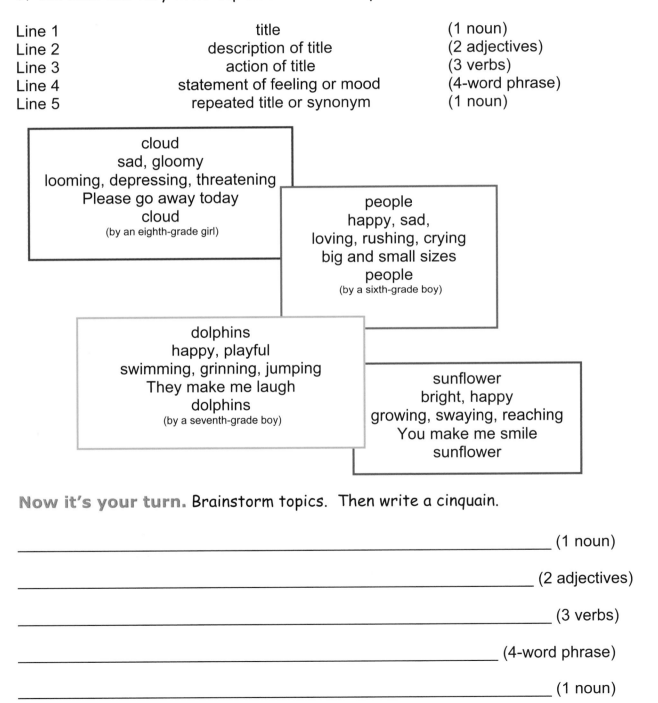

cloud
sad, gloomy
looming, depressing, threatening
Please go away today
cloud
(by an eighth-grade girl)

people
happy, sad,
loving, rushing, crying
big and small sizes
people
(by a sixth-grade boy)

dolphins
happy, playful
swimming, grinning, jumping
They make me laugh
dolphins
(by a seventh-grade boy)

sunflower
bright, happy
growing, swaying, reaching
You make me smile
sunflower

Now it's your turn. Brainstorm topics. Then write a cinquain.

_____ (1 noun)

_____ (2 adjectives)

_____ (3 verbs)

_____ (4-word phrase)

_____ (1 noun)

Skill 3: A Diamante

A diamante (dee' uh mon tay') is a diamond-shaped poem of opposites. It does not rhyme. Notice that the last word in the poem is the opposite of the first word. Below is the pattern showing the parts of speech for each line. Watch line four; it is the pivot upon which the whole poem turns. The first two nouns in line four describe the first opposite; the last two nouns describe the last opposite. The orange words in the pattern belong to the first opposite. The green ones belong to the last opposite.

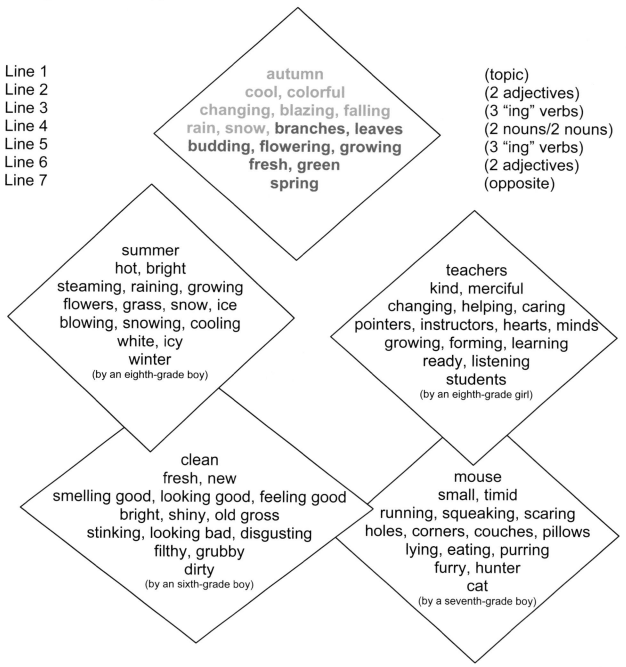

Line 1   autumn   (topic)
Line 2   cool, colorful   (2 adjectives)
Line 3   changing, blazing, falling   (3 "ing" verbs)
Line 4   rain, snow, branches, leaves   (2 nouns/2 nouns)
Line 5   budding, flowering, growing   (3 "ing" verbs)
Line 6   fresh, green   (2 adjectives)
Line 7   spring   (opposite)

summer
hot, bright
steaming, raining, growing
flowers, grass, snow, ice
blowing, snowing, cooling
white, icy
winter
(by an eighth-grade boy)

teachers
kind, merciful
changing, helping, caring
pointers, instructors, hearts, minds
growing, forming, learning
ready, listening
students
(by an eighth-grade girl)

clean
fresh, new
smelling good, looking good, feeling good
bright, shiny, old gross
stinking, looking bad, disgusting
filthy, grubby
dirty
(by an sixth-grade boy)

mouse
small, timid
running, squeaking, scaring
holes, corners, couches, pillows
lying, eating, purring
furry, hunter
cat
(by a seventh-grade boy)

Now it's your turn. Brainstorm pairs of opposite words. Then choose a pair. In the diamond shape below, put one opposite on the first line and the other on the last line. Finish writing your own diamante.

Pairs of opposite words:

1.

2.

3.

4.

5.

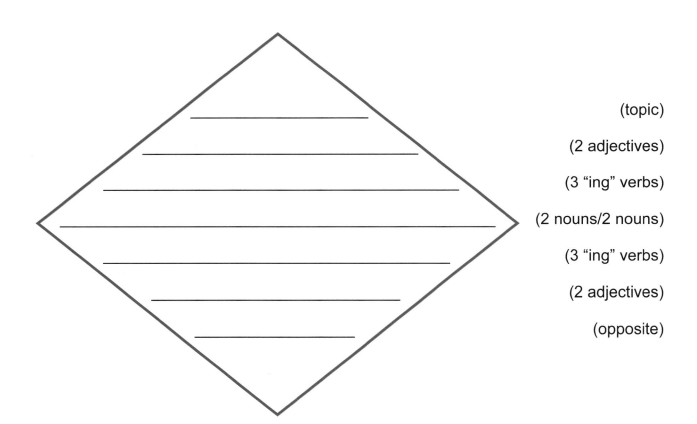

(topic)

(2 adjectives)

(3 "ing" verbs)

(2 nouns/2 nouns)

(3 "ing" verbs)

(2 adjectives)

(opposite)

Skill 4: **Limericks**

Limericks come to us from Ireland. They are happy and silly poems that have a definite **rhythm**. The first two lines have three beats. The next two lines have two beats. And the last line has three beats. Read the limerick below. The beats (*rhythm*) are underlined for you. When you read this poem out loud, put more emphasis on the underlined words.

Limericks also have a **rhyme scheme** (a pattern of rhyming words). The *rhyme scheme* is marked for you on the right of each line below. The first word at the end of a rhyming line is always labeled *A*, and anything that rhymes with that is also labeled *A*. The next word at the end of a rhyming line that doesn't rhyme with the A word is labeled *B*. Anything that rhymes with this B word is also labeled *B*. The next rhyming word that does not rhyme with either A or B is labeled *C*, and so on. However, there are no Cs in a limerick.

> **All limericks have the same rhyme scheme: A, A, B, B, A.**

There <u>was</u> a new <u>king</u> of the <u>Nile</u>	A	3 beats
Who <u>sat</u> in his <u>boat</u> for a <u>while</u>.	A	3 beats
But he <u>hung</u> out his <u>toes</u>,	B	2 beats
And as <u>everyone</u> <u>knows</u>,	B	2 beats
He was <u>lunch</u> for a <u>sly</u> croco<u>dile</u>.	A	3 beats

Now it's your turn.   Write a limerick. Follow the rhyme scheme and beats.

_____ (A, 3 beats)

_____ (A, 3 beats)

_____ (B, 2 beats)

_____ (B, 2 beats)

_____ (A, 3 beats)

Skill 5: A Hymn

Hymns are songs to or about God. People have been singing hymns for thousands of years, but the ones you sing on Sunday mornings are probably, at the most, only 300 years old. All of the Psalms in the Bible were meant to be sung. Some have even been rewritten into hymns that rhyme.

Verses for hymns usually contain two to four lines and use a variety of rhyme schemes (AABB, ABAB, ABBA, etc.). Many hymns, especially those of two lines per verse, include a chorus to sing at the end of each verse.

Now it's your turn. Below are the first verses (stanzas) of two familiar hymns. Underline the beats. The first lines of both hymns are done for you. If you sing the songs, it will be easier to feel the beats. Write the rhyme scheme on the blanks at the ends of the lines.

My <u>Je</u>sus, I <u>love</u> Thee, I <u>know</u> Thou art <u>mine</u>.   _____

For Thee all the follies of sin I resign.   _____

My gracious Redeemer, my Savior art Thou.   _____

If ever I loved Thee, my Jesus, 'tis now.   _____
                    (by William Featherstone)

A<u>ma</u>zing <u>grace</u>! How <u>sweet</u> the <u>sound</u>   _____

That saved a wretch like me!   _____

I once was lost but now am found,   _____

Was blind but now I see.   _____
                    (by John Newton)

Now it's your turn again. Write a hymn of at least two verses. Consider composing original music or using another hymn's music for your new hymn.

A suggested writing schedule:

Days 1-3   ❑ Write a new hymn. Set it to music if you wish.

Day 4   ❑ Sing or recite your hymn aloud.

Skill 6: **Copy** Cat

One of the best ways to learn how to write anything is to imitate a successful writer. When you imitate how authors write, you become more aware of the process and the patterns they use.

The same is true of poetry. You can choose a poem that you like and imitate it. How? It's easy.

Read the original poem. Underline the beats. Letter the rhyme scheme. Then write your own poem using the original poem's beats (rhythm) and rhyme scheme. Here are a few poems that are easy to imitate:

1. "Old Ironsides" by Oliver Wendell Holmes
2. "The Raven" by Edgar Allan Poe
3. "A Visit from St. Nicholas" by Clement Clarke Moore
4. Any nursery rhyme

Have you ever read "Old Ironsides" by Oliver Wendell Holmes? It has three stanzas (sections or verses), two beats to a line, and a rhyme scheme that usually rhymes only every other line. What is the poem about? Mr. Holmes wanted to save a ship that was due to be destroyed. It had been an important ship in the War of 1812, a part of American history. If you imitate this poem, you may want to write about something that is worth saving, something that people today don't think is very important.

Many people like the rhythm and the interesting rhyme scheme of Edgar Allan Poe's "The Raven." It's a lot of fun to read out loud. Here's the first stanza of that poem:

> Once upon a midnight dreary, while I pondered, weak and weary,
> Over many a quaint and curious volume of forgotten lore —
> While I nodded, nearly napping, suddenly there came a tapping,
> As of someone gently rapping, rapping at my chamber door.
> "'Tis some visitor," I muttered, "tapping at my chamber door:
>   Only this and nothing more."

One of the fun things about this poem is that it not only rhymes at the ends of some of the lines but it also rhymes in the middles and ends of other lines. In the first line, *dreary* and *weary* rhyme. In the third line, *napping* and *tapping* rhyme.

Turn the page for more examples of poems.

Probably one of the most imitated poems is "A Visit from St. Nicholas" by Clement Clarke Moore. Even radio ads and television commercials like to imitate Mr. Moore's famous poem as they sell their products. Here are the first two lines:

'Twas the night before Christmas, when all through the house
Not a creature was stirring, not even a mouse…

Check out this for an imitation of the beat and the rhyme scheme:

'Twas the day of the circus, when all through the town
No performer was stirring, not even a clown…

Nursery rhymes are interesting to imitate too. Their rhythms and rhymes are so familiar that they are easy to use in a poem of your own making.

Now it's your turn. Choose a poem. Use one mentioned in this lesson or find one on your own. Imitate its rhyme scheme and rhythm.

A suggested writing schedule:

Day 1　　　　　　　　☐ Read some poems and choose one to imitate.

Days 2-3　　　　　　　☐ Write a new poem based on the one you chose. Imitate the beats and rhyme scheme.

Day 4　　　　　　　　☐ Proofread three times. Make a neat copy. Read it aloud.

Skill 7: O, say can you…**What?**

Believe it or not, the national anthem of the United States was just a lowly poem until someone put it to music. When Francis Scott Key wrote the poem "The Star-Spangled Banner," he did not write the music for it. He may not have even intended his poem to be a song. But people liked the poem so much that they quickly put it to music—the music of an old drinking song first published in London in 1771 by a British man named John Stafford Smith!

Today it is hard to separate the words of the national anthem from its music. They seem to be woven together. But what if you could hum the tune and put new words to it? What would you come up with?

John and Charles Wesley often took popular tunes of their day and put new words to them. The new song combinations became some of the hymns we sing in our churches today.

You can do the same thing too. You can take the tune of any song and write new words to it using the built-in beat and rhyme scheme. Below is a silly example of new words put to an old song. Sing it to the tune of "Yankee Doodle":

> Sticky, globby, gooey mess
> Glued with something phony.
> They threw it on my plate at lunch
> And called it macaroni.

Now it's your turn. Create new words (lyrics) to fit an existing tune.

A suggested writing schedule:

Day 1   ➡ Listen to some songs or music and choose one to write new lyrics for.

Days 2-3   ➡ Write new lyrics for the tune.

Day 4   ➡ Sing or recite the new song aloud.

YOUR LOCKER

(Helpful Resources for Students)

Writing from Beginning to End

Brainstorm. Write down ideas. If your teacher lets you choose the topic, list things you know a lot about or are interested in. If your teacher chooses the topic, write down all the different possibilities inside this topic.

Narrow down your ideas. You can't possibly use all of them in your assignment. Keep the ones you can use and cross out the rest. Sometimes you won't know which ones to keep until you begin to research or write.

Make a list, outline, cluster, or Greek temple of all the ideas you intend to keep, putting them in a logical order for your paper.

Begin writing. Use the list you just made. Begin wherever you want to but remember to include an introductory paragraph, a new paragraph for each point, and a conclusion. Don't worry about mistakes. Write now; fix later. This is your first draft. Some call it a rough draft or a sloppy copy. <u>Never</u> hand this in to your teacher as your finished assignment.

Set your paper aside for a few hours or days. This means you won't be able to wait until the last minute to write it. When you set it aside, you are giving it time to cool off so that you can do the next step with a level head.

Reread your paper. By now, you will see some mechanical mistakes (commas, spelling, capitalization, and so forth). You will also notice some mistakes in how you said things. You will think of better phrases or sentences. Did you leave out a word? Did you misuse a word? You may want to move a whole sentence to another place. Maybe you will want to cross out some sentences and put others in. Fix your paper! Use **Mistake Medic** on the next page.

Proofread it. Comb through your paper. Look for all sorts of mistakes. Look for them one sentence at a time. Read your paper out loud. Resize the font. Proofread it from a printed copy, not from the screen. You will be surprised how many mistakes you find when you do these things.

Write your paper again. Make it as polished and as neat as possible. Before handing it in, read it one more time—slowly—to look for mistakes.

Hand it in and smile. If you have done all these steps well, both you and your teacher will be proud of your work.

Mistake Medic

1. Reread your paper:
   - Does it have an interesting title?
   - Does the opening sentence or paragraph grab the reader's attention by making a point, stating a fact, using a quotation, telling a story, or asking a question?
   - Does your paper get to the point quickly?
   - Does it stick to the point?
   - Is there a logical progression from one point to the next?
   - Is it easy to read and easy to understand?
   - Does the conclusion give the reader something interesting to think about?

2. Check your title for correct capital letters. Don't underline it or put quotation marks around it. Skip a line after the title.

3. Is your paper double-spaced?

4. Did you indent (five spaces) the first line of every paragraph?

5. Read your paper aloud. Is anything confusing? Add words or change them as necessary.

6. Look for unnecessarily repeated words. Use specific adjectives and nouns and powerful verbs, but don't get fancy.

7. Look for run-on sentences and sentence fragments.

8. Make sure all your commas are there for a reason, not just because you want to pause or have to hiccup. Check your other punctuation in the middles and at the ends of sentences. Refer to your grammar book.

9. Check your capital letters. Every sentence begins with one. Every proper noun needs one.

10. Circle possible spelling mistakes and homonym mistakes (*there, their*, and *they're*, for example). Then look them up in a dictionary.

11. Try these **tricks** to catch more mistakes. You will be surprised how many more you will find:
   a. **Print your paper** instead of proofreading it at the computer screen.
   b. **Resize the font** or choose another font. This moves the words into new positions, making it easier to catch mistakes you would normally read over.
   c. **Read your paper out loud** and listen to what you are saying.
   d. **Read each word**. Don't skim.

Hot Proofreading Tips

Read your paper out loud. You will be amazed at how many mistakes you can catch this way!

Ask a friend to read your paper. He or she may find something that doesn't make sense.

Resize the font. That moves everything around so you can see any mistakes quickly.

Label your sentence structures to make sure you haven't used the same ones over and over again.

Count the number of words in each sentence. Put the numbers in the margin. If all the numbers are similar, consider varying some of your sentence lengths.

Print out your paper instead of reading it at the screen. When you read the hard copy, you will find more mistakes.

DON'T LIST for Persuasive Writing

(from "Persuasion: The Basics," Skill 9, pages 44, 45)

1. **Don't insult** or single out a person or an entire group.
Wrong: Did you teens even look at yourselves in the mirror before you left the house? You're a mess!

2. **Don't wander** off your subject.
Wrong: I hope the library buys *Out of the Dust* by Karen Hesse. I read a lot of books. Just last week I read four books from the Left Behind series and two by Frank Peretti. Those men sure are good writers. I want to read more by them.

3. **Don't contradict** yourself.
Wrong: The team sure could use me at first base. That's my favorite position unless I'm playing shortstop.

4. **Don't go on and on.** Keep it short and sweet.
Wrong: Putting a statue in the middle of our park was so stupid. I mean, who needs another statue? We already have four around town. Why do we need one more bronze hero up on a horse? Our town will get a bad reputation for all the statues we have, and no one knows who those guys are anymore.

5. **Don't use "I think…,"** "I believe…," or "It is my opinion that…."
Wrong: It is my opinion that abortion is wrong. **Right:** Abortion is wrong.

6. **Don't write without evidence;** don't exclude facts.
Wrong: Probably some other towns have recycling bins too. I can't think of any right now, but I'm sure there are some.

7. **Don't be vague.**
Wrong: I want to talk to you about a problem in our town. It has been here for a long time. Everyone is bothered by it. Can't you see how bad it has gotten in the past year? Isn't it awful? And now it's time to do something about it.

8. **Don't be illogical;** don't draw the wrong conclusions.
Wrong: No one waited on me, even though I was there first. I know it was because of my red hair and freckles. The employees must hate red hair and freckles. They waited on two blondes before they would even look at me.

9. **Don't use jargon** (lingo) or technical words that only a few know.
Wrong: Be sure to attach the widget to the doohickey just under the spanner.

10. **Don't threaten** your audience or rant and rave.
Wrong: If I were you, I would watch out from now on! The next time I go into your red-hair-and-freckles-hating store, I'm going to do some damage! You'll see. You can't ignore me and get away with it.

DO LIST for Persuasive Writing
(from "Persuasion: The Basics," Skill 9, pages 45,46)

1. **Do treat** your reader intelligently.
Right: Teens, please show that you respect yourselves by dressing modestly.

2. **Do talk fairly** about the opposing view.
Right: Many women say that abortion is an important part of women's rights. They want to be able to make decisions for themselves about their bodies. And that seems logical until you realize that there are a lot of little girls who will never have any rights because someone made the decision of death for them.

3. **Do quote** people or experts or the Bible.
Right: I'm the right person for the first base position. Even Coach McGraw said last year, "If you want first base done right, rely on Pat. Nobody's better."

4. **Do be clear** about your topic.
Right: When I finished reading *Out of the Dust*, I knew other teens would like it. That's why I hope the library buys it.

5. **Do identify yourself** if it adds to your topic.
Right: I don't want the new highway to go through Vine Street. I should know. I've lived there all my life. **Right:** I am a frequent babysitter, so I know the importance of first aid training.

6. **Do define** your terms.
Right: Open your bumbershoot (umbrella) with care.

7. **Do know your audience.** Know their age, gender, interests, and so forth.
Wrong for a newspaper: Various personages subscribe to the fortuitous vicissitudes of existence. (This means that some people believe in chance, but it is too wordy for a newspaper, which is normally written on a 12-year-old reading level.)

Wrong: If you write a letter to the editor of your city's newspaper about how your church should have blue hymnals instead of red, you will be forgetting that most of the readers don't attend your church.

Right: When you write that article on friendship for *Brio* magazine (published by Focus on the Family), you will write it for Christian girls who are 12 to 16 years old.

Right: When you give your Christian testimony in church, you use words and phrases that everyone there understands. But when you give your testimony to a friend who is not a Christian and who hasn't ever been to church, you will use words that he understands. You will mean the same thing, but you will use different words.

Different Ways to Write Biographies
(This list is also in "A Biography," Skill 2, page 102.)

1. Write about a person's accomplishments: If he hadn't been born, then we wouldn't have _____ (or we wouldn't know _____).

2. Write about the part of his childhood that is the key to his future accomplishments.

3. Write about the life of someone you respect. Use her accomplishments and difficulties to show why you respect her.

4. Write about the life of someone you don't respect. Don't choose a family member or neighbor! Choose a person from history or a person in the public eye today. Write about his negative accomplishments or his character flaws to show why you don't respect him.

5. Write a "Who Am I?" in which you tell interesting things about the person but save the name for near the end of your biography.

6. Write about an important or pivotal day in the life of your person. Show what happened and how it changed him.

7. Write about a person's spiritual development throughout his life.

8. Write an imaginary page from your person's journal, diary, or letter. Show the reader what your person was like. Include facts.

A Book Response

(This list is also in "A Book Response," Skill 1, pages 129,130)

ARTISTIC SKILLS

1. **Draw, paint, or sculpt** an interesting character or scene from the book. Label the work or include a caption.

2. **Create a mural** with friends. Illustrate a setting or a scene.

3. Make a **3-D scene** in a box (a diorama) to illustrate a section of the story. Use the author's description of that scene. Try to capture the mood too.

4. **Draw a map** for the inside cover of the book, labeling the lands that people in the story traveled in. If it is a journey, show the beginning and the destination. Don't forget the dangerous places. Color your map if you want to.

5. Research the kinds of clothes (or weapons, houses, cars, furniture, etc.) the people in your story might have used. **Draw or paint** pictures of them, **build** a model or replica, or **sew** the clothes.

6. **Act out** an important scene from the book with a friend or two in front of an audience. Use costumes and props.

WRITING SKILLS

7. Make a **report card** for the author. Grade him on the basics: setting, characters, plot, etc. Also grade him on how he began and ended the book, if the book held your attention, if he used similes and metaphors, etc. Include why you gave him those grades and what he can do to improve.

8. Write a **story or poem** of your own based on something you read in the book.

9. Write a **letter to the author.** Ask something about the book or mention what you learned from it. If the author is still living, you can send your letter to the publisher listed on the inside of your book.

10. Write a letter to an **imaginary librarian** telling her why she should buy this book for the library. Include a little bit about the book, why it will appeal to other readers, and why you liked it.

11. Write a **blurb** (the part of the story you find on the back cover of the book). Tell enough of the story to get the reader interested—but don't tell the ending!

12. Write a **negative blurb** as on the backs of A Series of Unfortunate Events books, telling the reader why he should <u>not</u> read the book. This is using reverse psychology. The more you tell the reader not to read it, the more he will want to.

13. Write a pretend **telephone conversation** between you and a friend. Tell her why you think she would like the story and what you liked about it. Or warn her about it and say what you *didn't* like.

14. Read about any **animals** in the book and write a short report or give a short speech on them.

15. Write a **television commercial** for the book. Include what you liked about it. Then read it to an interested audience.

Notes

Notes

Notes

Notes